THE NIXON YEARBOOK 1968

Published by
Nixon Publications
Committee

"THE DICK NIXON I KNOW..."

In May of 1958, during an official tour of South America by Vice President and Mrs. Nixon—a mission which on the whole was highly successful—they were twice attacked by Communist-led mobs. They were shoved, stoned, and booed, and on one occasion the car in which the Vice President was riding was smashed. Full reports were of course cabled to the White House by others in their party, and I was so delighted with the remarkable conduct of the Nixons in this shocking affair that I sent the following message to Dick:

"Your courage, patience and calmness in the demonstrations directed against you by radical agitators have brought you new respect and admiration in our country."

During all the years I have known Richard Nixon, I have had occasion to observe many times the qualities mentioned in that cablegram. He is a composed man, not easily ruffled by events, and he seems always to have had the courage of his convictions and the patience to work tirelessly toward the goals he believes in.

No one can review the record without becoming aware of the great trust I placed in Vice President Nixon and his high level of performance throughout my eight years in the White House. Time after time, I asked him to undertake tasks, both domestic and foreign, of the utmost importance and delicacy. Moreover, in the major crises of those years he was one of a group of advisers with whom I took counsel. His progressive attitude coupled with his good sense, his keen mind, and his willingness to think and act on his own were enormously helpful to me on innumerable occasions.

In one of my campaign speeches prior to the 1960 election, when Nixon was so narrowly defeated by John F. Kennedy, I asked the question: "What qualities must the next President have?" Then I gave what I felt was the proper answer: "Character, Ability, Responsibility, Experience." And I added that the then Republican candidate possessed these qualities.

I have not changed my mind during the intervening years.

There is one other quality of Dick's I wish to mention: His loyalty to his party—the party that sent him to the House of Representatives, then to the United States Senate, and finally elevated him to the Vice Presidency. He is a fighting campaigner, and he has never hesitated to give unstintingly of his time and energies in behalf of other candidates—even when he himself wasn't running for office. This also is a quality I like.

These are a few of the reasons why I am for Dick Nixon for President.

D. E.

BY
DWIGHT D. EISENHOWER

A TESTING TIME FOR AMERICANS

"Have we the will, the moral and spiritual drive to take charge of our destiny once again, to regain the momentum and the leadership that was ours after our victories in World War II?"

I say the real and permanent grandeur of these States must be their Religion. Otherwise there is no real and permanent grandeur
WALT WHITMAN

We are embarked, we Americans, upon a great adventure, a demanding voyage from which there can be no turning back. For better or worse, the future of mankind depends on how we as a nation manage the trusteeship of power which has been placed in our hands.

From the beginning, implicit in the whole American adventure has been the sense that we were building a nation not for ourselves alone, but as a beacon to mankind, a land that held the hope and promise of the rainbow. More than ever before the nations of the free world need such a beacon and such a hope. But they no longer look to the United States as the unquestioned champion of freedom and progress. The American right to leadership is in question, and this is a challenge we must meet.

To meet it we must take new courage: courage to grow, courage to change, courage to lead once again. There are hazards in such a course, and there are hardships. But we must embrace them. For a nation's energies do not thrive in a vacuum. Nations and individuals *need* challenge; they *need* to have their strength tested in order to discover their reach and their staying power.

The world is undergoing a storm of change that affects all peoples and all societies, and we in this country are in the eye of this social hurricane. How we direct our lives and our national fortunes in the months and years just ahead will determine our country's future for the rest of this century. We have the manpower and the material resources to enter now on the greatest period of growth any nation has ever known. The question is whether we have the will, whether we have the moral and spiritual drive to take charge of our destiny once again, to regain the momentum and the assurance of leadership that were ours after our victories in World War II. We have lost some of our vigor and some of our confidence. Only if these are restored can we meet our moment in history.

For generations, America was a new nation in an old world. Suddenly we have become an old nation in a new world. We are a battle-scarred veteran and the young countries are looking us over. They want to know if we still have those qualities that have made us great. I say we have, and this is the time to prove it. This is a testing time for Americans.

We face enormous tasks, both at home and abroad. In a sense, these are extensions of one another.

Abroad, we must bring peace to a warring world; at home, we must bring peace to a warring society. Abroad, we must bridge the gulfs between the have and have-not nations; at home, we must bridge the gulfs between the have and have-not parts of our own population. Both at home and abroad we must break down the racial barriers that set man against man. These challenges, foreign and domestic must be met at the same time. For unless we win peace abroad, whatever progress we make at home could go up in the smoke of a disaster enveloping the entire planet. Unless we win peace at home, we will lose the respect of the world and our rightful place in it.

Our message to the peoples of the world is and must be one of hope and assurance. We must declare that there is a way to cast off the shackles that have crippled mankind; we must insist that the conditions of life in most of the world today can be changed. And we must carry this message even more with deeds than with words.

Our government represents the people of the United States, but it must also speak to the people of the world—just as our whole society must. But unless we can speak confidently and proudly, unless we can speak from a platform of social order and social progress at home, we cannot expect our words to get a hearing abroad.

There are great tasks ahead—and great goals to reach. Fortunately, we have the tools to work with. Man's resource of will is the greatest natural resource the world possesses. No energy source tapped by science will ever be a substitute for human willpower. When driven by a sense of necessity, a sense of survival, men and nations can perform monumental tasks, and they can overcome seemingly impossible obstacles.

The challenge that faces America today is no less than one of survival. Everything we stand for as a nation, everything we have lived for, fought for and died for is being tested every day. Our ideals of democracy, our standards of fair play, our belief in human freedom and human equality are being questioned. People at home and abroad are beginning to ask, "What has happened to America?"

What *has* happened to America? Over the recent years a great deal has happened. We have become bogged down in a war that we could have won years ago. We have allowed a climate of lawlessness, and violence, and crime to grow to intolerable proportions. We have allowed racial tensions to increase nearly to the breaking point. We have allowed a virulent inflation to infect our economy. We have allowed many things to shift us off our proper course. As a result, there has been an erosion of pride in America and in being American, an erosion due in part to the feeling that our hopes for our country and for mankind are not being realized.

Instead of moving ahead with the American program, we seem to be floundering. There are rumbling undercurrents in our society — undercurrents which often are crosscurrents. Vast numbers of people feel that society has left them, or that they want to leave society; they feel alienated, out of tune with America's ideals, or with their conception of those ideals. Vast numbers of people are looking for inspiration, for direction, for an answer to the question, Where is America going?

A large part of this unrest stems from the fact that as the government grows in power and scope, the role of the individual grows smaller, giving rise to a general feeling of helplessness and uselessness. All of us, unquestionably, are suffering from too much government. This is nothing new in the world. It has happened to other countries before. But this is the first time it has really happened in the United States of America, and it has weakened our society; it has undermined our sense of individual responsibility.

If we are to restore our lost pride and our old vigor, if America is to resume her rightful and essential role in the world, Americans—all of us—will have to acquire new self-discipline. We will have to shoulder more responsibility. The job of being an American citizen in 1968, 1969 and in the '70's is going to take guts, gumption and good hard work. It's going to take everything we've got, but I know Americans, and they've got enough of what it takes to start any job that needs doing and to finish any job they start.

It is essential for each one of us to realize that whatever we as a nation achieve, whatever we produce, will be done by our own energies and inspiration. Only to the extent that we can marshal these energies and encourage this inspiration can we succeed in any of the goals that we set for ourselves.

As we look across the sweep of this final third of the century, the one thing on which all else in America depends is the restoration of the place of the individual in the structure of our society. The people are the base on which our government is built, on which our society is built, on which our economy is built. The greatest glory of our nation is that the nation exists for its people, not the other way around.

And this is tomorrow's frontier: the frontier of man himself. We are approaching a golden new age, potentially more glittering than any man has known or, except in his wildest dreams, imagined. Never has so much trained intelligence been concentrated in one nation. Never have such vast forces been under man's control. Never have there been available such extensions not only of man's muscle, but of his mind —extensions that can at last make possible the full realization of man's potential. But before these potentials can come to flower, there must be a new place and a new role for the individual in American life.

If America is to be true to its destiny, true to its future, true to its promise, we must restore the sense of a driving dream. The American dream has been one of extraordinary power—precisely because it is rooted in the innermost strivings of man's spirit. It grows out of a sense of the inviolate dignity of the individual, and of the immense potential of the free human spirit. More than 100 years ago, Ralph Waldo Emerson said, "I sing the infinitude of the private man." To release these energies and develop these infinite potentials is the continuing challenge of America.

Richard Nixon stands out among all of the presidential nomination candidates of both the Democratic and Republican parties as the man who should be the next President of the United States.
—SHREVEPORT, LA., *The Shreveport Times,* June 16, 1968

NIXON NOTES

Change is the essence of progress. But there can be no progress without order, no freedom without order, no justice without order.

Only if we can make substantial progress toward balancing the federal budget are millions of Americans going to be able to balance their family budget.

When inflation sets in . . . the consumer takes a beating; the administration takes a powder, the farmer takes the rap.

The man who sits silent while society's laws are being openly violated is silently collaborating with the enemies of that society. And the nation which accepts public lawlessness as a legitimate means of dissent has passed a significant milestone on the road to anarchy.

My philosophy has always been: don't lean with the wind. Don't do what is politically expedient. Do what your instinct tells you is right . . . The politician who sways with the polls is not worth his pay. And I believe the people eventually catch up with the man who merely tells them what he thinks they want to hear.

Whenever we have tried to purchase peace at any price, the price has always been an installment payment on a bigger war.

I believe that historians will record this: That in the watershed year 1968, America, in a time of crisis, responded as it has responded before—with new ideas, great traditions, a new alignment, and with the fresh hope that comes from a new unity.

I have supported the 18-year old vote since the proposition was first suggested. The reason is not because they are old enough to fight. It is because they are smart enough to vote.

Never before has a generation of under-25 Americans felt itself so estranged from the rest of our society, so alienated and isolated.

Crisis in Denver—October 8, 1955.
*Vice President Nixon leaves hospital
after visiting stricken President
Eisenhower. With him is heart
specialist Dr. Paul Dudley White,
White House Press Secretary
James C. Hagerty and Presidential
Assistant Sherman Adams*

THE WHITE HOUSE

WASHINGTON

Denver, Colorado.
October 1, 1955.

Dear Dick:

I hope you will continue to have meetings
of the National Security Council and of the
Cabinet over which you will preside in ac-
cordance with the procedure which you have
followed at my request in the past during
my absence from Washington.

As ever,

Dwight D. Eisenhower

The Vice President,
Washington, D.C.

RICHARD M. NIXON

At 55 years young, in robust health and in exuberant spirits, Richard M. Nixon is a living example of the American Dream

RICHARD M. NIXON

Family Portrait—*In Buster Brown haircut, Richard (right) and brothers Harold (left) and Donald pose with parents Francis A. and Hannah Milhouse Nixon*

Richard M. Nixon: The Record

Richard M. Nixon will be his party's choice for President in 1968.

He has been for over twenty years one of the most widely-known and talked-about political figures in the United States.

What is this man's record? What have been his accomplishments? What have been the major events of his political and personal life?

Since 1946, when he first entered Congress as a representative from the twelfth district in southern California, through his years as Vice President in the Eisenhower Administration, to his current position as his party's choice, Nixon has a record unique for activity and high performance:

He was Vice President of the United States from 1953-1961. He was the second youngest man in history (at age 39) to hold that office.

In the last twenty-two years Mr. Nixon has won five out of seven election contests. He served in the House for four years and in the Senate for two.

At 55, Nixon is younger than President Lyndon B. Johnson, Governor Nelson Rockefeller of New York and Vice President Hubert Humphrey.

He is currently senior partner in one of the largest law firms in the country, a position he was named to in 1963 after practicing law in Los Angeles for two years.

He is probably the most extensively traveled man among major political figures of our day. In the last five years he has visited Vietnam five times, and, since 1961 he has traveled abroad 14 times, visiting every continent, and making three round-the-world journeys.

In February, 1968, Richard Nixon announced his candidacy for the nomination of his party for the office of President. He entered Republican primary elections in six states and won them all. The victories were all the more impressive because of the vote percentages in each state: in New Hampshire he received 79 per cent of the vote; in Wisconsin, 80 per cent; in Nebraska, 71 per cent; in Oregon, 73 per cent; and, in South Dakota and in Indiana, 100 per cent of the vote.

This is part of the man's record. But who was this man? Where did he come from? What is his background? Who are the people around him?

Family Portrait—*In Buster Brown haircut, Richard (right) and brothers Harold (left) and Donald pose with parents Francis A. and Hannah Milhouse Nixon*

Birthplace—*The modest frame home in Yorba Linda, California, where Richard was born on January 19, 1913*

Man and Boy—*The former Vice President at six months, three years and eighteen. At far right, in his Whittier high school football uniform after a rough game*

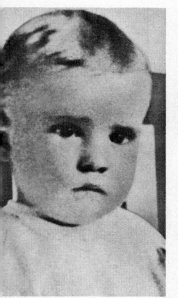 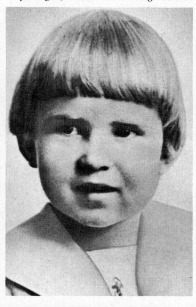  

Quiet Reflection—*California's new Republican Congressman, aged 33, visits the House for the first time in his new capacity January 3, 1947*

Proper Attire—
*The Nixon lads in
Yorba Linda. From left:
Richard (9), Harold (12),
Arthur (4), and (in tire)
Donald (7)*

Responsibility—*8 year old Richard
takes baby Arthur out for a ride*

Pause in the
day's occupation—
*At age 13 Dick
worked part time and
summers in his father's store
and filling station*

14

Muse—*The young violinist
was 15 at the time this picture
was taken and a sophomore in high
school. Dick still retains his
love for classical music*

Chums—*RN and friends in Whittier*

Lost Confidant—
*Richard's older brother
Harold (right) died in 1933
in his 23rd year*

Undergraduate — Richard (center) with Whittier College classmates

Whittier Squad — The young man (circled) with his college football team is still, today, an avid fan

Young Attorneys — The Duke Law School Class of 1937. Barrister Nixon, top row right

The Early Years

He was born January 9, 1913 at Yorba Linda, California, the son of Francis A. and Hannah Milhous Nixon. When he was 9, the family moved to Whittier, California, where his father ran a general store and a filling station.

Mr. Nixon's mother was a Quaker and the tenets of that faith have played a major part in the Nixon story. A belief in the virtues of hard work (he worked in the family store as a boy) and a strong desire for peace and true social justice, both part of the Quaker philosophy, have been part of his life since his days in Yorba Linda and Whittier.

He attended the local high school and then worked his way through Whittier College, a small Quaker school, where, after a student career in which he was elected president of his class and became a champion debater, he received a B.A. in 1934. In that year he received a scholarship to the law school of Duke University where he once more was elected president of a student organization, this time the student bar association.

He returned to Whittier, where he practiced law four years. In 1940, Mr. Nixon married Patricia Ryan, a Whittier school teacher, daughter of a Nevada miner.

At the advent of World War II, Mr. Nixon joined the Navy and served three and one-half years, rising in rank from lieutenant, junior grade, to lieutenant commander. He spent most of his naval career in the Pacific.

The Man and His Family

The Nixons have two daughters, Patricia, 22, a recent graduate from Finch College in New York, and Julie, 20, a student at Smith College. Julie is engaged to David Eisenhower, grandson of the former President.

The family lives in a ten room co-operative apartment on Fifth Avenue, overlooking New York's Central Park, in the same building in which Governor Rockefeller has a residence.

Since he became a senior partner in his law firm, Mr. Nixon has made approximately $200,000 a year, from practicing law and from writing. The law firm— Nixon, Mudge, Rose, Guthrie, Alexander and Mitchell—has a staff of seventy lawyers, serving many international and corporate clients. Their offices oc-

RICHARD
M. NIXON

South Pacific—
*Navy Lieutenant Nixon (3rd
from left) served 15 months
with South Pacific Combat Air
Transport Command, rose to
Lieutenant Commander*

Duty Bound—
*The young naval officer
ready to ship out for the
Pacific Theatre*

cupy four floors at 20 Broad Street in the heart of the financial district in New York City.

Mr. Nixon himself is an ardent sports fan, attending games whenever he can, and always following baseball and football through the sports pages. For relaxation he likes to listen to classical and semi-classical music and to play the piano. Formerly a golfer, Mr. Nixon now gets his exercise by walking; his doctors say he is in robust good health.

He is one of the few men in American public life who writes his own speeches. He keeps up with current events by wide reading and by discussion with friends in the business, governmental and academic worlds.

Mr. Nixon's public career includes the following:

The Years in Congress

In 1946 the twelfth congressional district in California was represented by Representative Jerry Voorhis who had held that office for ten years. Richard Nixon, 33, unseated this veteran Democrat by winning the election by a margin of 15,592 votes, with 56.7 of the total vote.

He became a member of the House Education and Labor committee where he helped to draft the Taft-Hartley labor law of 1947.

As a member of the Herter select House committee, he visited Europe in 1947 and helped to build the foundation of America's post-war foreign-aid programs, beginning with the Marshall Plan.

In 1948 Mr. Nixon won the nomination not only of his own party but also that of the Democratic party and was re-elected with 141,509 out of 162,807 votes cast.

After four eventful years in the House, Mr. Nixon chose to run for the Senate seat left vacant by the retirement of Senator Sheridan Downey, a Democrat. Mr. Nixon handily defeated Mrs. Helen Gahagan Douglas with 59.2 per cent of the vote and by a plurality of 680,947 votes in a state where Democrats outnumbered Republicans 3 to 2.

Throughout his congressional career, Richard Nixon was an advocate of and voted for legislation supporting: the United Nations, foreign aid, military assistance for European allies, the North Atlantic Treaty Association, and technical assistance for underdeveloped areas.

He has opposed the admission of China into the

Back in Civvies—
*candidate Nixon
in his first campaign
(California, 1946)*

Mutual Admiration—
*The new Congressman
escorts his mother to 1946
campaign victory party*

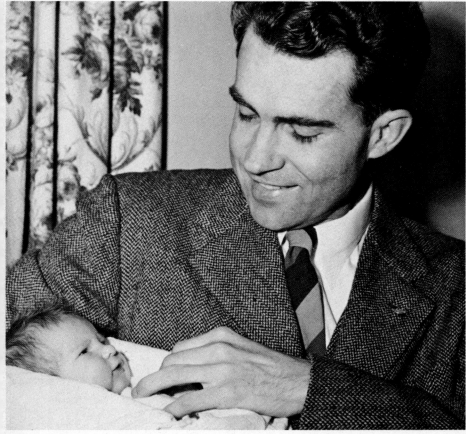

Daddy—*Enter Tricia on February 21, 1946. She was one day old when this picture was taken*

Grecian Arrival—*The Herter Committee in Athens. From left: Congressmen Mahon (Texas), Nixon (Calif.), Jenkins (Ohio) and Richards (S.C.)*

Senatorial Victory—*After only two years in the House, powerful vote-getter Nixon was his party's and the California people's choice for Senator*

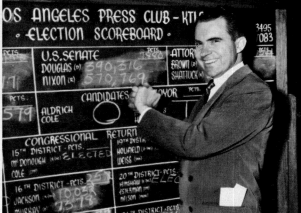

Cherub and Cherry Blossoms— *A happy Congressman and his lovely spouse take Tricia for a spin*

GOP Nominees—1952

Faithful Aide—*Rose Mary Woods, Mr. Nixon's executive secretary when he first became Vice President is still with him today*

Foursome Fun—*President Eisenhower, Vice President Nixon, John Eisenhower and Attorney General William Rogers at Burning Tree Country Club*

Inspiration—
Old friend, Evangelist Billy Graham breakfasts with Vice President

Capitol Respite—
The young Vice President takes a bit of sunshine on the steps of the nation's Capitol

Friends—*Vice President Nixon and then Senator John F. Kennedy stop to chat during 1960 presidential campaign*

Crisis in Caracas—*Guard surveys smashed windows of automobile in which the visiting Nixons were attacked by communist-led mobs, May 4, 1955*

Unanimous Acclaim—*The President and Vice President acknowledge delegates' cheers in 1956 after being unanimously nominated for re-election*

United Nations.

In domestic affairs, Congressman Nixon supported civil rights, increased Social Security benefits, statehood for Alaska and Hawaii, and the raising of the federal minimum wage.

He voted against the extension of federal rent controls and against poll taxes and segregation in the armed forces.

The Vice-Presidential Years

In 1952, at the age of 39, Richard Nixon was chosen by acclamation to be the running mate of Dwight D. Eisenhower at the head of the Republican ticket.

In 1956, Mr. Nixon was once again called upon by his party to run as Vice President on a ticket headed by President Eisenhower. In 1952, the Eisenhower-Nixon ticket won by a plurality of 6,621,242 votes, receiving 55.1 of the total vote; in 1956, the Eisenhower-Nixon victory assumed even larger proportions: a margin of 9,567,720 votes with 57.4 of the total.

Nixon as Vice President

He and his wife visited 55 countries on good will visits as the personal emissary of the President. In 1958, during an historic tour of nine South American nations, the Nixons were stoned and attacked by communist-led mobs in Peru and Venezuela.

In 1959, Mr. Nixon visited Poland and Russia. In Russia he engaged the Soviet Premier, Nikita Khrushchev, in the now-famous "kitchen debate" which brought international attention to the Vice President when it was televised world-wide.

As presiding officer of the United States Senate, Mr. Nixon broke more tie votes than any other Vice President in history.

He also presided over Cabinet meetings, and, during the two illnesses of President Eisenhower in 1955 and 1956, presided over meetings of the National Security Council. Mr. Nixon served as head of two intergovernmental agencies: The President's Committee on Government Contracts and the Cabinet Committee on Price Stability for Economic Growth.

Of Mr. Nixon, President Eisenhower said: "No man in history was ever better trained for the Presidency."

Historic Moment—*There are three Presidents and a potential President in this rare picture taken at the 1957 inauguration. Standing solemnly for The Star Spangled Banner are Presidents Truman, Eisenhower, and Hoover. Vice President Nixon is in foreground. Behind President Truman is John Eisenhower*

RICHARD M. NIXON

The Record

In seven election contests (the 1968 contest will be his eighth), Mr. Nixon lost two:

In 1960, running for President (with Henry Cabot Lodge as his running mate), Richard Nixon was defeated by John F. Kennedy (with Lyndon Johnson as vice-presidential candidate) in the closest national election in 76 years . . . a difference of one tenth of one per cent of the vote proved to be the difference between defeat and victory for Richard Nixon in 1960. The popular vote for Kennedy-Johnson was 34,226,731; for Nixon-Lodge, 34,108,157.

Mr. Nixon carried 26 states; Kennedy carried 22. (Two were carried by the late Senator Harry F. Byrd of Virginia.)

Mr. Nixon returned to California after his defeat. There, in 1962, he ran against Governor Edmund "Pat" Brown for the office of Governor of California. Nixon faced a primary fight against Joseph Shell. He beat Shell in the primary election by 1,288,000 votes to 670,000, but went on to be defeated in the election by Governor Brown. The result: Brown got 51.9 per cent of the vote, beating Mr. Nixon by 296,758 votes out of 6 million votes cast.

The Years Since 1963

Mr. Nixon's life as a member of his law firm has been as varied and exciting as his life as a member of government. The many outstanding events of the last five years have included argument before the Supreme Court of the United States.

But even with his heavy schedule of law work, Mr. Nixon found time to travel and speak on behalf of the Republican Presidential nominee of 1964, Senator Barry Goldwater. In 1966 Mr. Nixon made campaign appearances for Republican candidates in 35 states and in 61 congressional districts. His appearances were credited by most observers as being the major factor in the Republican resurgence of 1966.

In 1967, Mr. Nixon visited over 40 countries in Africa and the Middle East, Europe, Latin America and Asia, and the Soviet Union.

After his complete sweep of the primaries in 1968, it was evident that Richard Nixon had made one of the most remarkable political comebacks in the history of American and/or World politics.

NIXON NOTES

It is time to move past the old civil rights, and to bridge the gap between freedom and dignity, between promise and fulfillment.

If we really want to do something about our dollar, the thing to do is not to keep Americans from spending more abroad but to get this Administration to spend less at home.

No man can predict the ultimate shape of the new alignment that is happening in America today. But I know this: It is alive, it is moving forward, it is rooted in reality, and it calls out for you to come aboard.

To the young people of America today, I say this: It's true that you are inheriting a world you never made. But this was also true of every generation. The great, exciting difference is that you live in a world you can change.

In a contest of promises, the man who promises to spend has a clear edge over the man who promises not to spend. The appeal of the spender today is to those people who do not stop to think.

When respect for America falls so low that a fourth-rate military power like North Korea dares to seize an American naval vessel on the high seas, then I say it's time for new leadership in Washington—leadership that will restore respect for America around the world.

A man who never lost himself in a cause bigger than himself has missed one of life's mountaintop experiences. Only in losing himself does he find himself. Only then does he discover all the latent strengths he never knew he had and which otherwise would have remained ever dormant.

We must never forget the strength of America is not in its government, but in its people. There is no limit to the goals America can reach, provided we stay true to the great American traditions.

Partners—*At work and at play Pat and Dick Nixon share and share alike. In times of trial, triumph or travail, togetherness has marked their 28 years of married life. Here—at the helm of the Nixon family houseboat*

AND THIS IS HIS PARTNER: PAT NIXON

"What better credentials could one present to qualify for the post of First Lady?"

Any woman whose role it is to be the embellishment, buffer and bulwark of a good man can appreciate Pat Nixon's gratification last June 14th. That day, from the same school, Finch College, where daughter Tricia was receiving her B.A., Mrs. Richard Milhous Nixon was honored with a degree of Doctor of Laws. Dr. Roland R. DeMarco, president of the college, read the citation:

Patricia Ryan Nixon

You have distinguished yourself in public and private life. A scholarship student at and a cum laude graduate of the University of Southern California, a former high school teacher, a devoted wife and mother who has always striven to maintain the home as a quiet sanctuary for your family, a charming and very effective ambassador of good will on your many worldwide trips, and a champion of and worker for social causes including the Legal Aid Society. and the Boys Clubs of America.

The record is clear that you have performed each role with a self-effacing dedication, with great distinction and with obvious success. You are a living personification of the highest ideals of womanhood.

In public . . . where Dick's forthrightness has ever been complemented by her graciousness; where she has unstintingly exchanged a lithe and competent handshake with her husband's electorate — where, fronting the nation's cameras in times of great triumph, intense suspense or deep disappointment, Pat's fair facade has remained composed, confident.

And she is distinguished in her public life, by her acumen of the often edgy amenities of protocol. When Richard Nixon won the Vice Presidency, there had been no Mme. V. P. on the Washington scene for almost 7 years. Patricia, falling heiress to barely remembered, outmoded traditions, scrapped them respectfully, and minted her own. Since their residence was too modest to contain the elaborate "return dinners" tendered visiting chiefs of state, Pat sought historic sites, Blair House, Anderson House, the Pan American Union Building. She organized every detail—staff, service, linen and silver appointments, flower arrangements, guest lists, menus, music. She frequently chose a theme for such parties, thereby bringing rare fresh air to formerly stuffy ceremonial rites. She also introduced the idea of including women in the after-dinner discussion, thus eliminating the previous pattern of women stranded together engaging in small talk of weather.

Under the auspices of the Nixons, state occasions acquired a special scintillance and ease. At the urging of President and Mrs. Eisenhower (who thought "the young people do such a good job of it") Pat and Dick took on many social obligations which would have been within White House domain. Mrs. Vice President Nixon earned her place as one of the most responsible, popular and least maligned hostesses in capitol history. Patricia's obvious good will precludes other women's envy of her success.

And in Private Life . . . which the Nixons make such a masterful effort to *keep* private . . . the plans and progress of two unspoiled daughters are treated as seriously as Dick's political aims. Twenty-year-old Julie's engagement to 20-year-old David Eisenhower receives the maternal attention such a milestone would command in any family. Tricia's dates are greeted with charm and warmth which might be accorded an Ambassador. Dick's seclusion when he is engrossed in listening to one of his classical records is respected.

A non-participant in New York cafe society, a non-member of the boutique clique, Pat has kept up with her reading. She attends those art shows, concerts and plays which truly claim her interest.

The Nixon home (presently a 10-room apartment overlooking Central Park) is furnished in no particular period, but with a tasteful and comfortable lifetime accumulation of fond furnishings. Pat is pleased to rotate from storage to service accessories such as lamps, vases and bric-a-bric, bringing dear pieces to light again in new locations and arrangements.

Always prominently placed is the painting of an Indonesian landscape, a present from President Sukarno, and an exquisite "sumie" floral scroll, brushed and signed by Mme. Chiang Kai-shek. A gift to Julie, at present on loan in the Nixon living room, is a charming painting titled "Welcome to Gettysburg" by no less an artist than D. D. Eisenhower. It pictures in bloom the 50 trees from 50 separate States which line the driveway to the former President's home. Another original Eisenhower, Ike's gift to the Nixons, is of the chapel at Gettysburg under snow.

Pat's personal friends, like Dick's are not necessarily notables, but congenial, reciprocal confidantes who have weathered the test of time. It is indicative that Rose Mary Woods, Dick's longtime administrative secretary, falls into Pat's group of close friends.

"A scholarship student at and a cum laude graduate of the University of Southern California . . . a former high school teacher."

Patricia Ryan was born on St. Patrick's Day in Eli, Nevada, of a miner-father who turned rancher and

moved to Artesia, California. Pat's own girlhood was not exactly golden. After her mother died, when she was thirteen, Pat kept house for her father and brothers. Her father's death when she was seventeen loaded Pat with additional burdens, and forced her to work her way through school. This she did as bank teller, switchboard operator, movie extra, X-ray worker, salesgirl. That 'cum laude' was hard come by.

"I found out" she says, "that you can do anything you put your mind to. You can adjust to anything if you want to." After graduation from U.S.C., she went to Whittier, Cal. to teach school for four years—*and* to meet and marry a struggling young local lawyer. Pat's alma mater has subsequently awarded her a doctorate in Humane Letters. She has been offered many other honorary degrees but declined them while Dick was in office.

"As a devoted wife and mother who has always striven to maintain the home as a quiet sanctuary for your family."

A teamed integrity characterizes the Nixons as a couple. During the four years Dick spent as a naval officer, part of the time in the South Pacific, during World War II, Pat got a job in San Francisco—in the unfulfilled prospect of leave-time together. Since that era—22 of their 28 married years—Pat has shared Dick's public career as secretary, research director, and intuitive pollster of women's opinions. "I carry messages from the women to Dick," is the way she puts it. "What they are thinking and feeling...what they envision for their children." It is, perhaps, Richard Nixon's most important secret weapon that his wife is one of those fairly rare women who is on easy speaking terms with the rest of her sex. And registered women voters in the U.S. outnumber the menfolk by 4,000,000!

Pat takes the hectic pace of a campaign at an easy lope. For her a three day swing around three States is a cinch. After all, this is Pat, Dick's Partner, the gal who once went Friendship Tripping Around The World in *18* Days. She knows how to use every moment from touchdown to takeoff—and, airborne in their chartered jet, she'll grant an interview to one or two of the newsmen aboard, write "thank-you" letters to hosts at the last port of call, and jot notes for her talk before the Women's Club at the next stop.

When Dick is on the platform, her expressive brown eyes are on him. As he delineates the issues, she accords a characteristic small nod of approval. The fact is she shares Dick's convictions as an independent thinker, but also, most unshakably, as his spouse. In unending hours on a receiving line, she focuses her attention astutely and kindly on every comer. Posing under hot lights, she and Dick will have *individual* pictures taken with possibly 250 delegates and committeemen—a grueling ordeal which would send the most seasoned campaign wife to the showers in hysterics. But Pat is as poised and friendly and as genuinely concerned about the third person's appearance in the last photograph as the first. She has entered into a cheerful conspiracy with cameras, and she knows how to make not only herself but others look good.

As a *family,* the Nixons exemplify the very qualities which are Dick's prescription for America— unity, stability, achievement via action. These qualities are seasoned by love and respect. Unity shows in the girls' volunteer barnstorming on Dad's behalf. Julie and fiance David Eisenhower gave up their spring semester weekends from college to stump the Primary States. Tricia made her first solo appearance as a campaigner in Iowa on the Fourth of July.

No scandal, not even a rumor, has ever clouded the Nixons' domestic sky. After years under public surveillance, but much more importantly under the gentle persuasion and firm protection of their parents, Tricia and Julie emerge as promising young people of differently faceted personalities. What Tricia (The Thinker) and Julie (The Speaker) have the most in common are Dick and Pat's exacting credo of personal honesty, plus a mutual consuming interest in history. Tricia, with talents in historical writing, majored in history at Finch. Julie, entering her junior year at Smith College may well direct her interest in history toward producing documentary movies.

As a mother, Pat's efforts to maintain a "quiet sanctuary" are displayed in her insistence on a minimum staff. She performs every possible loving chore and skilled detail herself and has encouraged her daughters to do the same. "My children didn't get everything on a silver platter either," she says. "They've always been expected to work around the house or in the office. We live in an affluent society, but I really think it would be better if everybody kept busy." Sewing and cooking are regarded as creative essentials. Knowledge of proper laundering and

Little girls do grow up—*Pat, Tricia and Julie have been a closely knit trio, sharing books, pets, seashells. At the Nixons, every happy event becomes an Occasion and there is always that "big project" underway whether, as little girls, making a 5-room "decorator" house for kittens out of cardboard boxes or, as teenagers, constructing a king-sized scrapbook out of wallboard. (See selections from the latter made by Tricia and Julie for* The Yearbook *starting on page 40)*

AND THIS IS HIS PARTNER, PAT NIXON

White House Receiving Line—*A familiar duty for Pat, as President and Mrs. Eisenhower continued to expand the national, social and diplomatic duties of the Vice Presidential office. Of Mrs. Eisenhower, Pat says: "She was not only The First Lady in fact but a great and gracious friend to all"*

creaseless packing are musts.

Yet often the Nixon household veers from the quiet almost to the boisterous. This is thanks, in part, to the series of pets which have succeeded Checkers (the famous and beloved cocker spaniel long since passed away). Currently there is Julie's poodle Vickey, and Tricia's Yorkshire terrier Pascha. Things become nicely noisy when Dick, an accomplished "by ear" pianist, leads a community sing.

"A charming and very effective ambassador of good will on your many world wide trips . . ."

As President Eisenhower was dispatching his Vice President on an international mission, he added to Pat, "*You* go along too. Let the world get acquainted with a typical young American couple." So Pat went along and *not* just for the ride, and *not* just to be delightful at diplomatic dinner parties. She worked in hospitals, orphanages and homes-for-the-aged all over the earth. Together the Nixons logged 148,229 miles on official visits representing the President.

In the 60 countries the Nixons have visited, and they've visited many countries more than once, they've cut loose from the crowned heads and top brass long enough to tune-in with the people. They've been as lavishly received by heads of state, and as warmly by the people in their private citizen journeys as when they were Mr. and Mrs. V. P.

Pat recalls their reception on the Philippines Tenth Anniversary of Independence. A million Philippinos had come out to greet them. The sea of faces and waving arms stretched out into a floodlighted field. Long into the night the Nixons drove through the throng—cheering and grasping hands, physically, and fact-tually linking two great nations rejoicing in liberty.

Then, in contrast: early morning in Budapest, Hungary, when the Nixons slipped past the doors of their sleeping Iron Curtain hosts to go to the public market at opening time. First shyly, almost surreptitiously as the family was recognized, vendors came out of their stalls to present a plum, a cabbage, a bun. There was *almost* a cheer, as people came running with fine specimens of produce. One little boy tendered a peony from his grandmother's flower cart, was beamed on by Tricia, came back with more posies for Julie and Pat. Then he started bringing them on by bunches until the Nixons withdrew for fear of putting grandma out of business. Finally, the

exuberant marketeers hoisted Dick up on their shoulders and began carrying him around—at about the time the police arrived to "restore order."

Pat reminisces about the Khmer temple of Angkor Wat in Cambodia; over her visits to military hospitals in Hanoi while Dick was up at the front and the French were fighting in '56. To places most travelers don't go, the Nixons have gone with good will, and felt well-rewarded: Auckland, New Zealand; Asuncion, Paraguay; Khartoum in the Sudan; Libya; Uganda; Afghanistan, to name a few.

"And a champion of and worker for many social causes including the Legal Aid Society and the Boys Clubs of America."

How did it happen two organizations were singled out of so many causes which have benefited from Pat Nixon's participation? "Well, Tricia answered the telephone when the call from Finch came in and she thought that my efforts for Legal Aid might better recommend me to receive a Doctor of Laws," she explains. Then, "Dick's a National Director of Boys Clubs—but I've worked in the field—and I mean *real fields* for that one too. When I do charity work, I don't just lend my name. I get in there and work. I've done much PTA and a lot of Girl Scouting. I stay in touch with youth and I enjoy it too. I think today's young people *want* to have a purpose and be involved. I think what they most want is guidance and jobs. We have to see to it that they get them."

"The record is clear that you have performed each role with a self-effacing dedication, great distinction and success. You are a living personification of the highest ideals of womanhood."

What better credentials could one present to qualify for the post of First Lady? Style and social grace are part and parcel of Pat Nixon. But dignity, self-discipline and steadfastness are virtues in which she personally sets store and aims to maintain. In fact, if Patricia Ryan Nixon could be faulted on anything, it is over-perfectionism. At a rare loss for words, she makes exactly the right gesture—exactly right, well-timed and appropriately her own. As Pat gracefully mounted the rickety steps to a spotlighted stage in Cleveland, with thousands watching, a girl in the crowd was asking a friend, "How would it be now— if she broke her heel?" It was a typically feminine thought. Well, the answer is: it would be just great. Pat would make it great.

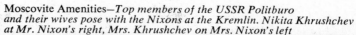

Mercy Call—
Pat Nixon's causes are legion. Here, as a Red Cross nurse she admires Presidential signature flag

Moscovite Amenities—*Top members of the USSR Politburo and their wives pose with the Nixons at the Kremlin. Nikita Khrushchev at Mr. Nixon's right, Mrs. Khrushchev on Mrs. Nixon's left*

Alaskan Romp—*Herb Klein, Pat Nixon and Rose Mary Woods set off for the ice country via dog sled. Rose is secretary to Richard Nixon and newspaperman Herb is Nixon communications chief*

Cheering Presence in Warsaw—*Pat has visited children's wards in hospitals all over the world*

Tiny Wave—*Pat adds to her many roles that of charming campaigner. Here, she greets crowd at Nixon rally*

Sea Stroll—*Pat and Dick always manage to steal some time from their crowded lives for themselves alone*

Richard M. Nixon

AMERICA AND THE WORLD

"If we are to regain our lost leadership there are three things we must do: We must see the world as it is, not as it was. We must face facts with a new realism. We must speak with a new candor."

The Great Kitchen Debate—*A dramatic moment as Vice President Nixon and Soviet Premier Khrushchev engage in a strong running debate on the Russian versus the American way of life during their tour of the American exhibition in Moscow in the summer of 1959*

Queen Elizabeth

Chancellor Konrad Adenauer—*West Germany*

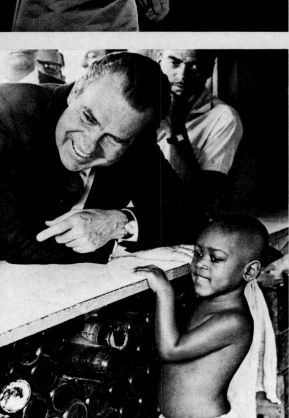

Encounter in Rio—*A Vice President makes friends with a Brazilian youngster in Rio de Janeiro during his South American tour in 1967*

Generals Walt and Cushman—*Vietnam*

Anyone who travels extensively abroad comes back with one indelible impression: Whether peace and freedom survive during this period will depend upon the leadership of the United States. Let us take an inventory of America's strengths and weaknesses as it attempts to meet this challenge.

Never has a nation had greater assets for leadership than those of the United States today. Our military power is awesome, our economic superiority unquestioned. Wherever we go, whether in Asia, Europe, Africa or Latin America, we find signs of the American presence and evidence of American influence. We have military bases around the world, fleets in every ocean; in every country there are sales offices and subsidiaries of American companies, and the movie house down the street is likely to be playing Hollywood's latest.

And yet, increasingly, we find signs of a paradox of American power: never has a nation possessed such power as the United States now commands, and never has a nation sought to use its power to nobler purpose—but seldom has a nation been so mistrusted in its purpose or so frustrated in its efforts.

The gap is widening between what our spokesmen say and what others believe.

The deficit in our balance of payments is matched by a mounting deficit in our balance of influence. Ideas should be our greatest export—and yet in the market-place of ideas, people of other nations are simply not buying American.

In our posture abroad, in our approach to the conduct of foreign relations, in our structure of alliances, in the terms in which we try to sell our ideas and our policies, America is succumbing to a creeping obsolescence.

Our example has lost its fire. Our leadership has lost its drive.

We are neither understood abroad, nor trusted. If we are to regain our lost leadership, there are three things we must do.

We must see the world as it *is,* not as it was or as we might wish it were.

We must face facts with a new realism.

We must speak with a new candor.

First, the world as it is. The most striking impression from months of travel is that we live in a new world. Never in human history have so many changes taken place in the space of one generation. Never

Prime Minister Eisaku—Japan
in his Tokyo office

Street meeting—Tunisia

has the pace of change been accelerating so rapidly.

It is a world of new nations—it is a world of new people. Half the world's nations have been born since World War II—and half the people now living have been born since World War II. To a remarkable extent this new generation has, as one Asian Prime Minister put it, "neither the old guilts nor the old fears" of the generation seared by war.

It is a world of new ideas. The old isms—communism, socialism, anti-colonialism—that summoned men to revolution after World War II, have lost their magic.

But while the new generation is no longer prisoner of the old isms, neither is it bowled over by American power or mesmerized by the American example. The young see the face of want and the face of hunger and the face of opportunity. Above all, they want change—change which will bring progress in solving these problems. Too often America appears to be the champion of the status quo rather than what we are —the boldest architects of change and progress civilization has ever known.

If our leadership is to be effective, we have to be believed. And in Europe, in Africa, in Latin America, in many parts of Asia, we simply are not believed. Nor will we be believed as long as we engage in sanctimonious sermonizing that irritates our friends, bores our enemies and leaves the cynical unconvinced.

Take foreign aid. Why have we given this aid? Because we are humanitarians, we like to say. Well, we are. But this isn't *enough* of a reason. And the world doesn't believe it.

Our aid programs are distrusted abroad for the same reason they're in trouble at home: because we have not frankly stressed the simple fact that by helping others we help ourselves.

If people are going to believe us when we say that our development aid is not the opening wedge of a new imperialism, they must be shown why their prosperity is in America's own interest.

And why is it in our interest?

America's basic self-interest in world development stems from the brutal fact that there can be no sanctuary for the rich in a world of the starving.

If present trends continue, the world's population will have been doubled by the year 2000—and seven-eighths of this increase will have been in the poor nations. The frightening fact is that the poor are multiplying twice as fast as the well to do. The greatest increases in population are among those who can least afford it.

However much it engages our compassion, the problem of hunger has to be met as a matter for the head, not just the heart. This means that if our aid programs are to play the role that they must play, then they must be drastically overhauled.

We ought to turn our aid programs more in the direction of stimulating private enterprise, less in the direction of financing government enterprise.

The economic history of the poorer countries since World War II points to one clear fact: that the successful countries have been ones that have adopted an incentive economy, while those that have followed the socialist road have failed. Where private development and government enterprise have been matched against one another, it has been the private program that has produced results.

We can realize the promise of the new world only by enlisting the resources of the old. But unless those resources are directed to reality—unless we "see it like it is," and "tell it like it is"—unless we strip away the wrappings of hypocrisy and speak with a new realism and a new candor, we may wake up to find that time and change have passed us by.

So let's stop apologizing for the success of free enterprise, and instead work at spreading and sharing those successes.

Let's stop apologizing for America's wealth and power. Instead let's use it aggressively to attack those problems that threaten to explode the world.

We *can* win the race with change. We *can* preserve our leadership. But to do so we have to recapture the faith and trust of a world in ferment. We have to revitalize the American dream, and cast it in terms that the new people of a new world can understand and appreciate and aspire to.

Whether their energies can be marshaled, their despair overcome, their hopes kindled, will largely determine whether the American dream can survive through the rest of this century. I believe that our dream will survive, and to make it survive and grow —at home and in the world—is the continuing challenge to American leadership.

President Kwame Nkrumah—*Ghana*

Emperor Haile Selassie—*Ethiopia*

Needed: A New Approach in Foreign Policy

We have come to a time when America must reappraise—in a most searching, measured and fundamental way—its role and its responsibilities in the world, and the resources which we and which other nations can bring to the meeting of those responsibilities.

We need to fashion a new diplomacy which can readjust the balances within the free world, as well as those between the free and the communist world.

Since World War II, the United States has moved into a new and unfamiliar position—often an uncomfortable position—of power and of responsibility. We have inherited by default the role of the world's chief keeper of peace and guardian of freedom. This is a role we did not ask; it is one history thrust upon us. But our not asking it makes it no less ours.

However, conditions have changed since we first assumed that role. The other nations of the West have grown in strength. Japan has moved into the first rank of industrial powers. All around the rim of China the nations of non-Communist Asia are building a new prosperity and developing a new cohesiveness, which together suggest that they should be able to play far more assertive roles in their own defense.

The Soviet drive for strategic supremacy—which the Soviets already have very nearly achieved, while the United States has passively watched—is deeply troubling and seriously threatening. No longer is it possible for the thinly stretched power of the United States to play the decisive role that it has in many crises in the past. Even where it can be deployed, it is not backed today by the decisive nuclear superiority which in the past has made it credible.

The United States has been able to keep the peace since World War II, as far as another world war is concerned, because we have had an overwhelming balance of power in our favor.

But we have let that balance slip, and with it we have seen an erosion of our ability to keep the peace in the world.

This has profound implications not only for the United States, but for the rest of the free world.

For one thing, it means that what has always been an elusive goal must now be made a reality. Economically, diplomatically, militarily, the time has come to insist that others must assume the responsi-

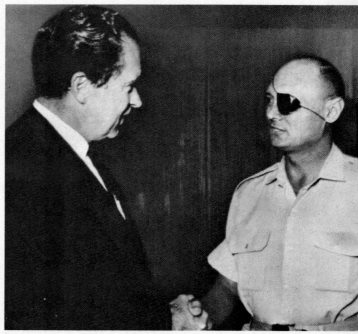

General Moshe Dayan—*Tel Aviv, Israel*

bilities which are rightly theirs. The other nations of the world must begin, and quickly, to pick up a greater share of the burden of the common defense.

To insist that others share more fully in the responsibilities of maintaining peace is not a retreat into a new isolation. Rather, it recognizes that today there are new realities of power. It recognizes, to put it very bluntly, that even if the United States had the will, it no longer has the capacity to do all that needs to be done. If the other nations of the free world want to remain free, then they must rise in their own defense. They can no longer afford the luxury of relying on American power.

We must, then, do three things. We must quickly enlist the other nations of the free world in the tasks which must be done. During this critical time of transition, we must continue to bear the burdens which are inescapably ours until a new system of stability can be constructed. At the same time, we must restore at least a part of the strategic advantage that we once held—not because we want power, but because in the world as it is we need power if we are to be secure.

Vietnam has been a deeply troubling lesson in the limits of U.S. power. But it is not enough simply to lament those limits, or to criticize the commitment, or to wish that history had dealt differently with that tormented part of the world.

The World We Live In

The crucial point is that we must confront the reality of the world as it is, even as we press toward the goal of what we want it to become.

The war itself is the latest and the grimmest battlefield in a larger, continuing struggle. This struggle is in part between the United States and the Soviet Union, and between the United States and Communist China, but more fundamentally between those nations that want stability and those that want instability; between those that want order, and those that want disorder; between those that want peace, and those that seek domination.

As we approach the day of nuclear parity between the United States and the Soviet Union, we approach the moment of truth in the relations between East and West. What strategists called the "Cuban power environment" no longer exists. In 1962, at the time of the Cuban missile crisis, the balance of strategic

power made it possible for President Kennedy to deliver a fully credible threat of nuclear retaliation. The balance was then sufficiently in our favor so that the Soviet ability to destroy the United States with an inferior missile force was doubtful, while the capacity of U.S. bombers and missiles to destroy the Soviet Union was certain. In these circumstances, the President was able to face down the Soviet leaders, and to force them to withdraw their offensive missiles from Cuba. But the United States no longer has such a decisive power advantage.

Nor do we command either the allegiance or the respect that were ours in the world at large only a few short years ago. No longer do our words receive the hearing they once enjoyed. Those who once *followed* the United States now *observe* the United States.

The world has lost much of its respect for our power. When we possessed an overwhelming strategic superiority, as well as mobile forces that could be dispatched to world trouble-spots both quickly and safely, without leaving other frontiers unguarded, then we had to be listened to.

Our ideals no longer communicate the fire, and the promise that they did only a few short years ago.

The world has lost its confidence in our dollar. It has lost its faith in our purposes, its respect for our judgment, its trust in our word. All of this indicates that we must develop—and quickly—a new approach in foreign policy.

If we delay our reappraisal of the U.S. role; if we delay moves to establish a new structure of security adequate to the age; if we delay these until the war in Vietnam has ended and the dust has settled, then—we will have delayed too long. Vietnam must be the last agony of the old order, because there is a question whether the old order could sustain another.

Both abroad and at home, the dominant trend of the middle third of the 20th century was toward the concentration of responsibility. What was needed now is a dispersal of responsibility.

The growing strength of the nations of Western Europe, of Japan, and of other nations now emerging into a new prosperity indicates the capacity of the noncommunist world to move toward a sharing of responsibility that accords with the new distribution of power.

Devising the most effective ways of achieving this is one of the central tasks of our time.

Tricia—*"Beachcombing on Key Biscayne. As far back as I can remember we have been a family of seashore enthusiasts. Give us sand and surf and salt spray and we're happy as clams"*

FAMILY ALBUM

Selections from Our Scrapbook, by Tricia and Julie

Julie—"With Daddy at the helm we're in good hands. I love this little glass boat. It's just great for sea-bottom searching—except when David pulls the drain plug and we join the fish "

Tricia—"The mild wild west. An unexpected overnight at the Jack Drowns when Julie and I only had party dresses to wear. So we borrowed these togs from Bruce and Larry"

Tricia—"A beloved puppet named Ralph whom Julie, then two, called Raf. Daddy was forever unscrambling the strings for us"

Julie—"The best part is the cake 'n ice cream. Birthday parties are my cup of iced tea. And at our house we'll throw one even if it's nobody's birthday. Tricia's the one who's grappling with her cake and I'm staring straight into the Brownie. We were six and four at the time"

Tricia—"Happiness is a warm puppy. When Checkers came to live with us and our kitten Nicky, Julie and I fairly burst with joy"

Julie—"The gal is shaking in her boots. This was the first time we met President Eisenhower. I was so awed that for the first time in my life I couldn't think of anything to say"

Julie—"A sandy time was had by all. This was at Ogunquit, Maine. I was too young to remember this vacation, but Tricia says we had a ball"

Tricia—"Split-level mansion for Nicky. This was one of Julie's construction projects with materials courtesy of the corner grocer"

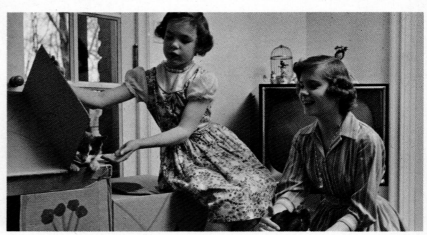

				BEL-AIR COUNTRY CLUB MEN								
			Donald	Jackson	Randy	Scott	Bebe Rebozo Doll	Klopp				
				Blue Tees SCGA Rating—72 White Tees SCGA Rating—71						WOMEN Red Tees WSCGA Rating—74		
YARDS	PAR	Stroke	Nixon	Jackson	HOLE	Scott	Rebozo		Stroke	PAR	YARDS	
468	5	9	5	5	1	5	7		13	5	437	
396	4	5	7	5	2	4	6		1	4	377	
155	3	15	1	4	3	2	4		15	3	126	
438	4	1	6	6	4	5	7		5	5	428	
123	3	17	3	3	5	2	5		17	3	103	
365	4	11	5	5	6	5	5		11	4	313	
379	4	3	5	7	7	5	6		3	4	346	
466	5	7	7	5	8	5	7		7	5	448	
331	4	13	5	5	9	5	7		9	4	318	
3101	36		44	45	OUT	38	54			37	2896	
218	3	6	5	5	10	4	4		18	3	105	
388	4	14	6	5	11	4	4		6	4	373	
382	4	12	7	6	12	4	6		4	4	355	
195	3	10	4	4	13	3	6		16	3	162	
575	5	2	6	7	14	6	8		2	5	536	
433	4	4	5	5	15	5	7		10	5	419	
189	3	18	3	3	16	2	5		12	3	166	
448	4	8	6	6	17	5	5		14	4	432	
378	4	16	5	6	18	5	5		8	5	365	
3201	34		47	47	IN	38	52			37	2915	
3101	36		44	45	OUT	38	54			37	2896	
6302	70		91	92	TOTAL	76	106			74	5811	
		HANDICAP							HANDICAP			
		NET SCORE							NET SCORE			

Labor Day Date 9/4/61   Scorer   Attest Dik N...

44   Tricia—"Daddy joins the hole-in-one club. He was so excited, he called us from the golf course to tell us about it. The other men in the foursome shown here are Donald Jackson, Randolf Scott and Bebe Robozo"

Julie—"Tricia was Sweet Sixteen and the cake was out of this world"

FAMILY ALBUM

Tricia—"Girl meets boy. Julie and David were both eight at the time. Our feeling is that this courtship must set some kind of record in the annals of romance"

Julie—"The V.P. Nominee and wife arrive home. This was right after the 1952 Convention and they brought us all kinds of wonderful souvenirs"

Julie—"Inaugural yawn. It was the 1956 Inaugural Ball of all places. But an eight year old lady—even in new white gloves—just can't take those late hours"

Tricia—"Highlight of a Roman Holiday. This was our first trip abroad with Mother and Daddy. We were 14 and 16. Pope Paul is the most gracious and impressive person we have ever met"

45

Julie—"Waiting for Daddy to come home. The man who took this picture won first prize in the 1952 annual White House Photographers' exhibition. We were four and six and my 'Tiny' doll was my constant companion"

Tricia—The cook has more help than he can handle. When he gets time to do it our family breadwinner is a wonderful chef

Julie—"When I was young and twenty! It had been raining all week but the weatherman relented on July 5th and gave me a beautiful sunny day as a birthday present"

Tricia—"Constitutional amenities! Mother and Dad return from a walk to Key Biscayne Lighthouse"

Tricia—"Julie gives her 20th Birthday acceptance speech. That night at her party our family musician took to the keyboard as we sang her a Happy" (see next page)

47

Richard M. Nixon

WE ARE GOING FORWARD

Toward Racial Peace
Toward a Law-Abiding Nation

"No candidate has addressed himself more realistically to the plight of the Negro slum dweller thus far in the 1968 campaign than Richard Nixon," said Time Magazine. "His philosophy combines pragmatism, compassion and faith in the black American's will to achieve his aims within the framework of society."

TOWARD RACIAL PEACE

Every age has its special set of problems, and every problem has its special catch-phrases. Today, we commonly speak of "the urban crisis." And yet the problems wrenching America today are only secondarily problems of the cities. Primarily, they are problems of the human mind and spirit.

Over and over again, we ask ourselves whether our cities can survive, whether they can remain livable, whether the races can co-exist within them, whether poverty and squalor must inevitably consume the inner city. In asking these questions, we are asking, in effect: how long can Americans ignore the race condition?

For years now, the focus of talk, of debate, of action, has been on "civil rights"—and the result has been a decade of revolution in which the legal structure needed to guarantee equal rights has been laid in place.

Voting rights, schools, jobs, housing, public accommodations—in all these areas, new laws have been passed, old laws struck down. And yet these victories have not brought peace, or satisfaction, or the fullness of freedom. Neither have the old approaches of the 30's—the government charities that feed the stomach and starve the soul.

No "More of the Same"

For too long, white America has sought to buy off the Negro—and to buy off its own sense of guilt—with ever more programs of welfare, of public housing, of payments to the poor, but not for anything except for keeping out of sight payments that perpetuated poverty, and that kept the endless, dismal cycle of dependency spinning from generation to generation.

Our task—our challenge—is to break this cycle of dependency, and the time to begin is now. The way to do it is not with more of the same, but by helping bring to the ghetto the light of hope and pride and self-respect.

I have said recently that the fiscal crisis now confronting America is so great, and so urgent, that only by cutting the Federal budget can we avert an economic disaster, in which the poor themselves would be caught calamitously in the undertow.

The reality of the national economic condition is such that to talk of massively increasing the budget in order to pour additional billions into the cities this year is a cruel delusion.

At such a time, it is gross irresponsibility to promise billions of new Federal dollars for the cities, or even for the poor. One thing worse than not keeping a promise is making a promise that cannot be kept.

But this does not mean that because we cannot do more of the same, we must do nothing new. Only those who are locked into the solutions of the past, who measure progress by billions spent rather than by results achieved, will let themselves be stopped by a budgetary wall.

Activating Our Resources

In the long run, I think history will judge it fortunate that the United States was forced by economic crises to turn to people, rather than government; forced to explore new and imaginative means of activating the real resources of America. For the plain fact is that all the money in the world wouldn't solve the problems of our cities.

We won't get at the real problems until we rescue the people in the ghetto from despair and dependency.

There's no pride at the receiving end of the dole, and until there is pride in the ghetto—personal pride and racial pride—we're not going to get anywhere in tackling the real problems of a real world.

Let me be very clear. As we look down this final third of the twentieth century, a period in which the population of our cities will double, the costs of both physical and human regeneration will increase greatly. No fiscal sleight-of-hand can restore and renew the cities without our having to pay the bill. And governments at all levels will have to join with private enterprise in meeting that cost.

What we do not need now is another round of unachievable promises of unavailable Federal funds.

The Bridges Needed Now

What we do need is imaginative enlistment of private funds, private energies, and private talents in order to develop the opportunities that lie untapped in our own underdeveloped urban heartland.

It costs little or no government money to set in motion many of the programs that would in fact do the most, in a practical sense, to start building a firm structure of Negro economic opportunity.

We need new bridges between the developed and underdeveloped segments of our own society—human bridges, economic bridges, bridges of understanding and of help.

One bridge is incentives to private industry to make acceptable the added risks of ghetto development and of training the unemployed. Helping provide these incentives is the proper role of government; actually doing the job is not—because industry can do it better.

Another bridge is the bridge of black success—a bridge that can be built only by those Negroes who themselves have overcome, and who by their help or their example can show that the way to the American Dream is not barred by a sign that reads, "Whites Only."

A third bridge is the development of black capitalism. By providing technical assistance and loan guarantees, by opening new capital sources, we can help Negroes to start new businesses in the ghetto and to expand existing ones.

Educational bridges can be built, now, at little cost—bridges of tutorial help, of business training, of remedial assistance, using volunteers who, in case after case, have shown themselves both willing and effective.

Bridges of understanding can be built by revising the welfare rules, so that instead of providing incentives for families to break apart, they provide incentives for families to stay together; so that they respect the privacy of the individual; so they provide incentives rather than penalties for supplementing welfare checks with part-time earnings, so that they are a temporary expedient, not a permanent way of life.

Welfare is something to be escaped from——not to.

The point about all of these bridges is that they can be built now; they don't require billions of dollars that the government doesn't have, and they don't require waiting until billions more become available. They are not the whole answer. But they are part of the answer—and a vital part, without which no amount of money can do the job.

These are the kinds of approaches that get directly at the matter of dignity and pride and self-respect; these are the kinds of approaches that can break the shackles of dependency, just as the laws of the past decade have finally broken the shackles of bondage.

Human Rights, Property Rights

Much in this area can be done through private initiative—for example, by groups such as John Gardner's forward-looking Urban Coalition. What they require is commitment, by private citizens as well as by public officials.

It's long been common practice among many to draw a distinction between "human rights" and "property rights," suggesting that the two are separate and unequal—with "property rights" second to "human rights."

But in order to have human rights, people need property rights—and never has this been more true than in the case of the Negro today. In order to enjoy the human rights that ought to be his, he has to acquire the property rights on which to build. What do I mean by property? Many things—but essentially, the economic power that comes from ownership, and the security and independence that come from economic power. Rights are never secure unless protected, and the best protections for a person's basic rights are those he can erect himself.

Black extremists are guaranteed headlines when they shout "burn" or "get a gun." But much of the black militant talk these days is actually in terms far closer to the doctrines of free enterprise than to those of the welfarist 30's—terms of "pride," "ownership," "private enterprise," "capital," "self-assurance," "self-respect"—the same qualities, the same characteristics, the same ideals, the same methods, that for two centuries have been at the heart of American success, and that America has been exporting to the world. What most of the militants are

All your strength is in your union,
All your danger is in discord;
Therefore, be at peace henceforward
And as brothers live together.
HENRY WADSWORTH LONGFELLOW

asking is not separation, but to be included in—not as supplicants, but as owners, as entrepreneurs—to have a share of the wealth and a piece of the action.

And this is precisely what the Federal central target of the new approach ought to be. It ought to be oriented toward more black ownership, for from this can flow the rest—black pride, black jobs, black opportunity and yes, black power, in the best, the constructive sense of that often misapplied term.

Black Enterprise

Philosophies, wars, power structures, all have turned historically on the basic questions of ownership—who owns the means of production, who owns land—for the simple reason that with ownership goes power, prestige, security, the right to decide and to choose.

We should listen to the militants—carefully, hearing not only the threats but also the programs and the promises. They have identified what it is that makes America go, and quite rightly and quite understandably they want a share of it for the black man.

For a long time, we too have been talking about preservation of the private enterprise system, about enlisting private enterprise in the solution of our great social problems, about profits as the great motive power of our fantastically productive economy. What many of the black militants now are saying, in effect, is this: "We believe you, and now we want a chance to apply those same principles in our own communities."

Our reply should not be to reject this request, but to seize upon it—and to respond to it.

The ghettos of our cities will be remade—lastingly remade—when the people in them have the will, the power, the resources and the skills to remake them. They won't be remade by government billions; the sad history of urban renewal, for example, has shown how often this results in an actual decrease in the number of housing units available for the poor, with one slum torn down and another created—because the basic conditions of slum life haven't been changed. These conditions are what we have to get at—the human and social conditions, the conditions of the spirit—and these in turn rest in large part on our laying in place the economic structure that can support a rebirth of pride and individualism and independence.

Free Enterprise in the Ghetto

For the individual, a job is the essential first step—whether toward independence, toward family responsibility, or toward advancement—but even jobs have to be provided within a framework that establishes dignity and the pride of the black man as well as the white.

It's no longer enough that white-owned enterprises employ greater number of Negroes. This is needed, yes—but it has to be accompanied by an expansion of black ownership, of black capitalism. We need more black employers, more black businesses.

Integration must come—but in order for it to come on a sound and equal basis, the black community has to be built from within even as the old barriers between black and white are dismantled from without.

We have to get private enterprise into the ghetto. But at the same time we have to get the people of the ghetto into private enterprise—as workers, as managers, as owners.

The Demand for Dignity

At a time when so many things seem to be going against us in the relations between the races, let us remember the greatest thing going for us: the emerging pride of the Black American. That pride, that demand for dignity, is the driving force that we all can build upon. The black man's pride is the white man's hope—and we must all, black and white, respond to that pride and that hope.

These past few years have been a long night of the American spirit. It's time we let in the sun.

It's time to move past the old civil rights, and to bridge the gap between freedom and dignity, between promise and fulfillment.

It's time to give a new dimension to our American concept of equal justice under law—time to give an answer of the spirit to America's crisis of the spirit—and it's a time to face our challenges not in despair but with zest—not with a heavy heart, not bowing sullenly to duty, but as an opportunity for America to redeem and enrich its heritage.

Ours is a chance today to change America, and, by our example, to help America change the world.

*The snow lying deep on
the earth dotted with young
pines, and the very slope
of the hill on which my house
is placed, seemed to say;
Forward!*

HENRY DAVID THOREAU

*"There is no shortage of ideas or programs or
tools or potential laws to deal with crime in this
country. The only shortage is a shortage of leadership that will place this problem in the first
priority of American business."*

TOWARD
A LAW-ABIDING
NATION

In the last seven years, while the population of this
country was rising some ten per cent, crime in the
United States rose a staggering 88 per cent. If the
present rate of new crime continues, the number of
rapes and robberies and assaults and thefts in the
United States today will double by the end of 1972.

That is a prospect America cannot accept. If we
allow it to happen, this nation will then be what it is
fast becoming—an armed camp of two hundred million Americans living in fear.

To stop the rising crime rate and to reduce the
incidence of crime in America, we must first speak
with a new candor about its causes and cures.

We cannot explain away crime in this country by
charging it off to poverty. The role of poverty as a
cause of the crime upsurge in America has been
grossly exaggerated—and the incumbent Administration bears major responsibility for perpetuation of
the myth.

On October 16, 1964, the President said that,
"The war on poverty which I started—is a war against
crime and a war against disorder." If the President
genuinely accepted that proposition, the nearly 50
per cent increase in crime rate since 1964 would be
adequate proof of the utter failure of the government's war on poverty.

The success of criminals plays a far greater role
in the rising crime rate than any consideration of poverty. Today, only an estimated one-in-eight crimes
results in conviction and punishment.

If the conviction rate were doubled, it would do
more to eliminate crime than a quadrupling of the
funds for any governmental war on poverty.

In short, crime creates crime—because crime re-

wards the criminal. And we will reduce crime as we
reduce the profits of criminals.

There is another attitude that must be discarded if
we are to wage an effective national war against this
enemy within. That attitude is the socially suicidal
tendency—on the part of many public men—to excuse
crime and sympathize with criminals because of past
grievances the criminal may have against society. By
now Americans, I believe, have learned the hard way
that a society that is lenient and permissive for criminals is a society that is neither safe nor secure for
innocent men and women.

No Sense of Urgency

The Administration seems to have neither an understanding of the crisis nor a recognition of its se-
verity. As a result, neither the leadership nor the necessary tools have been provided to enable society's
peace forces to regain the upper hand.

Organized Crime

Organized crime is the tapeworm of the American
society. In recent years it has prospered as never
before and broadened its influence in government,
legitimate business, and unions. The absence of an
adequate response at the national level — to this
national threat—is a glaring failure of the present
Administration.

One of the most effective groups of men within
government combating this kind of criminal activity
over the years has been the Organized Crime Section
of the Department of Justice. Yet, when President
Johnson took office, the number of man days spent
in field investigating by members of the OCS, the
number of man days spent testifying before grand
juries, and the number of man days spent in court
all suddenly decreased between 50 and 75 per cent.

This wholesale de-escalation of the Justice Department's war against organized crime has not to this
day been adequately explained.

Equally puzzling is the Administration's adamant
opposition to the use—against organized crime—of
the same wiretap and electronic surveillance the government employs to safeguard the national security.
Not only does the Administration oppose the use of
these weapons against crime, it has asked Congress

to forbid that use by law. Such legislation would be a tragic mistake.

Organized crime is a secret society. By denying to State and Federal law enforcement agencies the tools to penetrate that secrecy, the President and the Attorney General are unwittingly guaranteeing the leaders of organized crime a privileged sanctuary from which to proceed with the systematic corruption of American life.

Street Crime

But organized crime, though a multi-billion dollar enterprise and a major contributing factor to street crime, cannot alone explain the 88 per cent increase in muggings, robberies, rapes and assaults over the past seven years.

Another contributing cause of this staggering increase is that street crime is a more lucrative and less risky occupation that it has ever been in the past. Only one of eight major crimes committed now results in arrest, prosecution, conviction and punishment. Among the contributing factors to the small figure are the decisions of a majority of one of the United States Supreme Court.

The Miranda and Escobedo decisions of the High Court have had the effect of seriously ham stringing the peace forces in our society. The cumulative impact on these decisions has been to very nearly rule out the "confession" as an effective and major tool in prosecution and law enforcement, and thus to set free patently guilty individuals on the basis of legal technicalities.

The sight of guilty men walking free from hundreds of courtrooms across this country has not been lost on the criminal community.

I would thus urge Congress to enact proposed legislation that—dealing with both Miranda and Escobedo—would leave it to the judge and the jury to determine both the voluntariness and the validity of any confession. If judges and juries can determine guilt or innocence, they can certainly determine whether a confession is voluntary and valid. The rule of reason and justice should replace the Dickensian legalisms that have been obtained as a result of recent Supreme Court decisions.

If it should become impossible to draw such legislation to the satisfaction of the High Court, then consideration should be given to amending the Constitution. Involved here is the first civil right of every American, the right to be protected in his home, business and person from domestic violence, and it is being traduced with accelerating frequency in every community in America.

Leaning Too Far Backward

Wade and *Gilbert* are two other decisions of the Supreme Court, the extension of which have added to the problems of effective law enforcement. *Wade* and *Gilbert,* for the first time, ruled that in a line-up confrontation between witness and accused, the absence of a lawyer for the accused could, of itself, render the identification inadmissible in court.

My own view coincides with that of the dissenting minority, who expressed incredulity that a lawyer's presence at a line-up can somehow be helpful to the quality of the witness' identification. But *Wade* and *Gilbert* were carried to an almost ridiculous, if logical, extreme in U.S. versus *Beasley.*

(In the Beasley case, police observed three men beating and robbing an elderly man on the streets of Washington, D.C. When they approached, the assailants fled leaving their victim behind. Police gave chase and apprehended one man, and returned with him to the scene to aid the victim and radio for help. There was thus an inevitable confrontation between the suspect and the victim, and the former was positively identified by the latter as one of his assailants. The identification made on the spot was ruled as inadmissible evidence because the alleged assailant did not have an attorney present when he confronted the victim on the street, following the crime.)

These decisions by a majority of one of the Supreme Court have had a far-reaching impact in this country. They have been the subject of controversy; they were the focus of vigorous dissent on the part of the minority. And I think they point up a genuine need—a need for future Presidents to include in their appointments to the United States Supreme Court men who are thoroughly experienced and versed in the criminal laws of the land.

Strengthening the Peace Forces

A second major deficiency of the peace forces in this country is in the number and quality of the men who man the first line of defense—the police.

Today, two-thirds of the community police forces

in the country are undermanned. This year there will be 50,000 vacancies for police officers in the United States. To improve the caliber and increase the number of men who volunteer to fill those vacancies, the Federal and State as well as the municipal governments have a role to play.

The primary reason why there are not more and better police officers in our great cities today is quite simply that the rewards—economic and personal—of being a police officer have diminished sharply in the last two decades.

For many years, these men have been in effect increasingly subsidizing the communities which they serve—by accepting a wage rate that gradually fell behind other professions. From 1939 to 1966 while the real income of manufacturing employees in New York increased on the average of 100 per cent, that of a New York City patrolman increased by 20 per cent.

You cannot attract first-class men to do the difficult and complex and dangerous job of police work —if you simply give them a gun and $100 a week— which is the median beginning salary for patrolmen in our greater cities.

The responsibility for rectifying this situation rests largely with the municipalities and the people who live in them. They must be willing to pay the salaries to attract the kind of men they want standing between their property and family and the rising crime rate.

The Blue "Presence"

There is a considerable body of evidence to show that a dramatic rise in the number of patrolmen is followed by an equally dramatic drop in the rate of crime. The New York Subway system is a case in point—where the presence of a patrolman on every train at night brought a reduction of 60 per cent in the epidemic of juvenile terrorism in the first three months they were there. The lesson could be applied to dozens of other cities and communities across the country.

(Along these same lines, a judicious reallocation of existing police manpower can often have the same impact on crime as a numerical increase in the force. Systems Analysis can be used to reassign patrolmen from beats and areas where they are not needed to trouble spots. This is one way modern science has been and should be put at the service of justice.)

It would be difficult to exaggerate the urgency of the need for greater police presence—or the danger to the social order if we do not get it.

State Help

The State can assist the local community in improving the quality of its law enforcement agencies in a variety of ways. One of the most effective would be to use incentives to accelerate the trend toward larger and more efficient police units.

Today, there are more than 420,000 people involved in police work employed by 40,000 separate agencies. Many of these 40,000 agencies are tiny and inefficient municipal departments wholly inadequate to the tasks assigned them. Consolidation of many of these departments and their merger into city-wide or metropolitan-wide forces would give the peace forces a jurisdictional range and a level of strength more commensurate with the criminal forces—which ignore State lines, let alone the lines that divide tiny municipalities.

Federal Help

The Federal Government can play a leading role as well in furthering this objective of consolidating and reducing the number while improving the quality of law enforcement agencies in this country.

To do so, however, it will have to shift its emphasis from direct grants to local governments to block grants to the States. The former approach puts the Federal Government squarely into what must and should remain a local function—law enforcement. Direct grants for local police departments could bring domination and control and the door could be opened to the possibility of a Federal police force—a prospect we should avoid. Secondly, the block grant approach to the States will enable them to determine the priorities in the allocation of resources; and that, too, is as it should be. Third, this approach would strengthen the statewide police forces which are, by and large, efficient and professional organizations.

It would also enable the State to strengthen its own investigative and crime laboratory facilities, its intelligence, and records centers—which could be put at the disposal of local police. By providing the assistance to the States, we would strengthen law enforcement at a level at which it could deal more effectively with a criminal community that possesses a mobility and strength undreamed of a few years ago.

The Prison Problem

No national program for turning back the rising tide of crime can succeed if we continue to ignore a primary headwater—the prisons of America. No institution within our society has a record which presents such a conclusive case of failure as does our prison system.

A recent FBI study of some 18,000 convicts released in 1963 revealed that fully 55 per cent had been re-arrested for new offenses by June 30, 1966. Of those persons arrested on a new charge within 30 months, 67 per cent had been given a mandatory release by a penal institution.

In short—whether one believes that the purpose of a prison is to punish the criminal or to deter him from future crime or to rehabilitate him and guide him away from a career in crime—by either standard our prison system is a failure.

The American prison system needs to undergo a major overhaul—to be changed from a primary cause of the crime problem in this country into a partial cure. Stated simply and directly, the criminal rate in the United States would be a good deal lower if convicted felons were properly trained and equipped for reassimilation by the outside world.

Both Federal and State Governments share equally in the responsibility for changing our prisons into something other than an ever-normal pool of replacements for the criminal community.

Since, however, the Federal prison system houses only 10 per cent of the penitentiary population of about 200,000 its role will primarily be one of example, of assistance to the States, and of clearing legislative roadblocks to effective prison reform.

Recognizing a Mistake

During the depression years of the 1930's with millions of Americans jobless, many pieces of Federal legislation were enacted calling for discrimination against prison-made goods. It was assumed that conscripted labor inside a prison could produce goods at a far cheaper rate and thus enjoy an unfair competitive advantage over both free labor and free enterprise.

This legislation was always questionable, and one certain effect has been to deny to thousands of convicted men the type of work experience that might have given them the essential opportunity to find a job when they left prison. It is time that these existing legal barriers against providing convicts with the type of training and work that will give them a viable employment when they leave should be removed. According to the President's own Crime Commission, prison labor is no threat to free labor today.

Secondly, of the 120,000 people employed in correction today, five of six are employed in custodial or administrative work, leaving only some 24,000 in treatment activities to handle a combined jail and prison population of 400,000 and a total of some 1.3 million who pass through our system each year. That 24,000 figure includes all the psychiatrists, teachers, psychologists and social workers—and if we are serious about changing the results of prison life—then we have to be serious about increasing that number.

The necessity of other major reforms is equally obvious. A study of the prison population reveals that 50 per cent of it has only a grammar school education or less. Except for New York and California, prison education is provided by inmates—a majority of whom lack college degrees and many of whom are themselves without a high school diploma.

The number of parole officers dealing with that great segment of convict population that has been returned to society is also inadequate to its job. We are thousands of men away from achieving what is considered the desirable ratio of one parole officer to every 37 parolees.

To effect these reforms, to provide the personnel in terms of teachers, parole officers, psychiatrists, social workers, to change the American prison system from a pool of replacements for the criminal community into a system of effective correction and rehabilitation will require millions of dollars—whether taken out at the State or Federal level.

It will take not only more dedicated people, but new ideas and new resources and new tools if we are going to rebuild these broken careers and re-equip these men and women for useful lives.

These are not all of the steps that should be taken. But here, in these proposals, I believe a beginning can be made toward removing from this nation the stigma of a lawless society.

There is no shortage of ideas or programs or tools

or potential laws to deal with crime in this country. The only shortage is a shortage of leadership to place this in first priority of American business.

If the American people are willing to commit themselves to pay the necessary price to restore peace to the society, it can be done. If they are willing to commit themselves to the proposition that any man who disobeys the law pays the penalty the law exacts, then we can begin to turn this crime wave back.

In connection with the President's Crime Commission Report, a poll was taken of average Americans. It found that of those polled 43 per cent were afraid to be on the streets at night; 35 per cent would not speak to strangers, and 21 per cent used cars and taxis at night to avoid mass transit.

Those are not the statistics of a Great Society; they are the statistics of a lawless society—they are statistics we must and will change.

REMARKABLE COMEBACK

The rise of Richard Nixon to his present commanding position in the leadership of his party is one of the most notable achievements in political history

When a victorious Richard Nixon stood under the gleaming crystal chandeliers in the Grand Ballroom of the Benson Hotel in Portland, Oregon, he knew and thousands of his frenzied supporters knew that this victory marked the climax of one of the greatest political dramas in American history. He had trudged through the snows of New Hampshire, he had campaigned tirelessly up and down the American heartland of the Middle West. He had taken his case to the people telling them what was on his mind, answering their questions, letting them decide what role he was to play in the future of their country.

Now it was May 28, 1968–and the voters of Oregon had given him a smashing 73% victory in the Republican primary in their state. This was the final, sweet taste of glory that topped a string of brilliant Nixon victories in the 1968 Republican primary elections.

The record was there for all to read: Richard Nixon was the winner in every Republican primary he entered. And his victories were unquestioned and all but total. New Hampshire 79%; Wisconsin 79.7%; Nebraska 70.4%; Indiana 100%—and now Oregon.(In Pennsylvania, a favorite son state where Nixon was not on the ballot, 104,658 voters wrote in his name to give him a rousing 76.3%.)

The Gamble

Even before he decided to be a candidate once again for the Presidency, Nixon came to another decision—a courageous decision—that if he did run he would test himself, offering the best he had to the voters, and letting them judge his stature.

If he became a candidate, he said, "I will enter all the Republican primaries, and unless I win a majority of them I will withdraw from the race."

"No man who hasn't been tested in the fire of the primaries," he said, "no man who has not taken his case personally to the people of this country, deserves to be considered seriously as a candidate for the Presidency of the United States."

The reason Richard Nixon decided to take the hardest possible road to victory in the 1968 primaries stems from a part of his character that is deep within the man. Nixon is a stern taskmaster of himself. He will accept no compromise, tolerate nothing but what he knows is the best he can produce.

Richard Nixon loves his country. He has served it with great devotion and great ability ever since he

was elected to Congress in 1946. He believed in 1960 and in 1962 that he had a great deal to offer his country and his state. He still believed so in 1967, when he made his courageous make-or-break decision to test his strength in the primaries. If he won them all, and won them well, he would know and the people would know that he was the man in his party who had the best chance to win in November.

Now, as he stood in that hour of victory in Oregon, he looked back along the long and uncertain comeback trail. He was looking at one of the most amazing recoveries in American political life.

In 1962, the man who had been in Congress, a Senator, Vice President of the United States, with all the prestige and influence these positions carry, was now Richard Nixon, private citizen. How did this private citizen become in a few short years, his party's all but unquestioned choice for President in 1968?

Mysterious Progress

Unlike defeated championship prize fighters, world's statesmen do not fight their way back to the top: If it is to happen, a mysterious process must take place—one that draws them back into the arena. They are a part of that process, but they do not control it.

A nation has to need a certain type of man. That man has to have unique qualifications which no one else can quite match. If, then, there is a faltering of leadership at a time of crisis, a powerful pull will exert itself. Most important, these three elements, the man, the nation's recognition of his ability, and the nation's need, must come together at a given moment.

In 1921, Franklin Roosevelt, defeated as the Vice Presidential nominee and stricken with polio, was certain that he was finished in American politics. In 1929, Winston Churchill was turned out of office by his own party, which then proceeded to ignore him for ten long years. He was convinced his destiny was only to write history, never to make it. In 1946, Charles deGaulle resigned as President of France when the leftists gained power. In 1953, he dissolved his party and went into what he believed to be permanent retirement.

Against a Landslide

For Richard Nixon, the pull back to public life began almost imperceptibly. A chasm had developed within the Republican party in 1964, the most severe liberal-conservative split in half a century. A man of broad view and great stature was needed to begin to bring the widely-separated wings back to the body of the party. This Richard Nixon proceeded to do. In the 1964 campaign he travelled up and down the country and helped to prevent the predicted national landslide from permanently crippling the two party system by engulfing state and local candidates as well as the Presidential nominee.

Private Citizen

Throughout his years as a private citizen, Nixon travelled widely; in five years, he made overseas trips which were the equivalent of five times around the world. In more than 40 countries, he held discussions with the top leadership in government and business, seeking out information from decision makers about the strength and weakness of America's foreign policy. As a result of this hard and exhausting fact-finding, Nixon was generally conceded to be more authoritatively informed on foreign affairs than any other American in private life.

Meanwhile, as senior partner of one of the most prestigious law firms in the nation, Nixon was demonstrating his great ability in his profession. His fellow attorneys admired his erudition and the logic he brought to a case before the Supreme Court in which he defended the individual's right of privacy. His argument in this case, made without notes, impressed legal observers with his brilliance and its lucidity.

The Loyal Opposition

In 1965, as a heavily-Democratic Congress rubber-stamped the Johnson policy of heavy spending at home and gradual escalation abroad, a strong voice was needed to form the nucleus of an articulate and loyal opposition.

Increasingly, the responsible voice of Richard Nixon was heard taking stands that many did not yet want to hear: That enormous welfare programs were causing a runaway inflation and hurting most of the people that the programs were designed to help, that America was squandering its power in a piece-meal fashion in Vietnam, refusing to take initiatives that would shorten the war and win the peace.

Nixon was only slightly ahead of his time: by

1966, more and more Americans realized the wisdom of what he had been saying. With the Congressional elections in sight, hundreds of candidates asked him to come to their districts and focus attention on their campaigns. He went up and down the entire country, speaking out for Republican candidates. He began to give to the campaign the spark it needed. He had begun to come back, and while the country watched, he demonstrated what it takes.

Richard Nixon was the only public figure in the country to predict with what one journalist called "phenomenal accuracy" the result of the 1966 election: For the Republicans, net gains of 47 House seats, 3 Senate seats, 6 new Republican governors, and some 700 state legislators.

Fifty-five of the 82 candidates for whom he spoke won their races. Ten out of 13 senatorial candidates, and ten of the 12 gubernatorial candidates whom he publicly endorsed were elected.

Warren Weaver of the New York Times put it this way: "A G.O.P. candidate for whom Nixon did not campaign stood only a 45% chance of winning, while a man he embraced stood a 67% chance. It is hard to knock a coach who raises the team average that much."

When the 1966 election was over, the nation, the party and the opposition, knew that Richard Nixon was once again a man to be reckoned with in any consideration of Presidential candidates.

After such a heady experience as the campaign of 1966, it might have been expected that 1967 would be a time of political activity for Richard Nixon.

Instead, he made no move to capitalize on his 1966 victory. He withdrew from campaigning and left the field open to others — chiefly to Michigan Governor, George Romney, who was generally regarded the front-runner for the Republican nomination, and who vigorously barnstormed the country.

Nobody has been able adequately to explain what happened in the Nixon political story in 1967. His speeches and statements were thoughtful but infrequent; he was not running, yet his poll ratings were steadily rising. An organization formed to urge him to run found it easy to recruit volunteers.

In early 1968, the great confrontation was supposed to take place in the New Hampshire primary in March. George Romney took a hard look at his own polls, which showed Nixon winning by an im-

And everywhere increasing crowds—*as the former Vice President spoke out on the issues facing an agonized nation at home and abroad. As if by some mutual signal, the people of America—and particularly its corps of new voters—started a ground-swell of popular support that continued to expand Primary after Primary across the land. The time and the man of his times were exactly right for each other*

*Starr Rooter—Green Bay Packers quarterback Bart
Starr helped call winning signals for Dick Nixon in Wisconsin*

Reception Committee in Georgia

pressive 8-1 margin—and promptly withdrew from the race. The popular sentiment in New Hampshire was by no means anti-George Romney; it was simply enthusiastically pro-Nixon. After New Hampshire, the Nixon momentum began to be irresistible. With the victory in Oregon, the impossible goal that Nixon had set for himself had been reached: six primaries, six victories. A total of 1,600,000 votes—73% of all those cast! Significantly, in states that permitted Democratic voters to cross over and vote in the G.O.P. primary, write-ins by Democrats favored Nixon 3-1.

The Reasons Why

First, there is the man himself. There is no "new" Nixon; he has changed only by the normal amount a man changes and matures who spends six years studying, working, thinking. At 55—still the youngest of those mentioned for the Presidency in 1968—his sense of humor shows more, he seems more relaxed. As he himself put it: "Maybe those who speak of the new Nixon, didn't really know the old Nixon."

But there is a real difference in the context of his life and in his place in his country. The public takes one view of a man when he is driving ahead, striving upward, which was the Nixon of 1960. But it takes another and warmer view of a man whom the public calls back out of private life, when they need him to fill a void in national leadership.

No brilliant maneuvers and no manipulations, no expensive campaigns could have created that call and started that comeback. The man to fill that role had to be a man with a certain character and ability and the public had to know it needed just that man.

The man was one reason; and time was another. There are times when America can afford to take a chance on leadership, when America is willing to try the untested man. But there are other times—times of crises—when America needs a leader who has been tested and tempered in fires of great decisions, a man to inspire confidence, a man to reunite the people.

These are times of failure abroad and frustration at home, a combination of crises which has divided the nation as it has seldom been divided before.

The time is right for Richard Nixon; Richard Nixon is right for the time. That is the real reason behind the remarkable comeback. And in that courageous victory by an indomitable man lies the hope of a strong move forward, by a great nation.

Airport Press Impromptu—*As the Nixon campaign swept from New Hampshire into Wisconsin, cannonballed through Indiana, grew to an avalanche in Nebraska and South Dakota, and became a nationwide mandate in Oregon, Dick Nixon continued to draw unprecedented praise from the nation's press for his stand on the major issues*

New Hampshire 79%   Wisconsin 79.7%   Nebraska 70.4%   Indiana 100%   South Dakota 100%   Oregon 73%

Undisputed Champion of His Party—*At this moment in the history of the 1968 primaries Dick Nixon has won them all by unprecedented pluralities*

NIXON IN THE NEWS

The only avowed candidate for nomination for president of the United States who makes sense so far is Richard Nixon.

—Idaho Falls, Idaho, *Eastern Idaho Farmer,* May 23, 1968

While his detractors snicker, snigger and snort, Nixon is making some very sound and solid speeches.

—*New York Daily News,* April 23, 1968

Richard Nixon, for perhaps the first time in his career, really has charisma. People are eager to take his hand, or merely to touch him. He is at ease, and more than ever before he inspires confidence. A gentleman who can carry the first two primaries by four votes out of every five is clearly the hardest Republican for the Democrats to beat.

—RUSSELL KIRK, *The Indianapolis Star,* April 23, 1968

We believe Nixon a better man than he was in 1960 — more mature in speech and thought, considerably improved in manner and conduct, easier in his public relationships.

Nixon truly represents the center of the Republican Party which some say corresponds roughly to the political philosophy of classical liberalism.

Nixon can more than match Humphrey in experience, he knows the world and its problems as do few men, he shares liberal values but envisions their achievement in realistic ways.

—JOHN S. KNIGHT, *Chicago Daily News,* June 1, 1968

Nixon, as probably no other man in American public life, knows the ropes of politics and government.

He has not made any bloopers in his campaign. He would probably not make many mistakes as President. He would probably even be proof against the fatal transition period—the period when Lyndon Johnson, on the model of John Kennedy and the Bay of Pigs allowed himself to be saddled with the war in Vietnam.

—JOSEPH KRAFT, *The Washington Post,* February 26, 1968

Why do you want to be President?

Except for Presidents Truman, Eisenhower, and Johnson, I think I know perhaps better than any man in the country what a killing job the Presidency is. But at this time and place in our history, when the kind and quality of American leadership will determine not only the future of America but whether peace and freedom survive in the world, then I think it is necessary for any man who has the support of a substantial number of his fellow citizens, and the experience which might qualify him to be President, to enter the arena and try to demonstrate that he has those qualifications. That's why I went down the long, hard road of the primaries. That's why I'm taking on these questions. And only if, by my conduct of this campaign, I can demonstrate that I'm the best qualified man to lead America, do I want the job. If I *am* the best qualified, I do want it, and I'll do the very best job that I can—with the help of the American people.

Why are you running for office, after two defeats?

I gave a great deal of thought to that question myself before I made the decision early this year to become a candidate for President. I suppose I could paraphrase Gen. Douglas MacArthur's famous statement, which some of you older people will remember, when he came back from Korea. He said that old soldiers never die, they just fade away. I would say that old politicians, on the other hand, may die but they never just fade away.

Yes, I've suffered defeats. I suffered a defeat for the Presidency in 1960. I suffered a defeat for the Governor of California in 1962. I learned from those defeats. I think I'm a stronger man, and I would hope a better qualified man, for having gone through the fires of defeat than if I hadn't.

Now I don't want to leave any false impression here. I want to make it clear that I've *won* a lot of elections, too. And, having won some and lost some, I can say this: winning is a lot more fun. I want to win this time, and I expect to.

Please outline what you would do to reduce the increasing crime rate in the United States.

It is very difficult to answer that question briefly. Last May I put out a 6,000-word statement on crime.

I was glad to see that Congress passed a Crime Bill, which became a law in June.

But, briefly, these are the things that we need to do. For one thing, it's going to be necessary for us to pass legislation which will modify the effect of some of the Supreme Court decisions. Now, I want to make my position clear. As a lawyer, I've argued cases before the U.S. Supreme Court. I respect that court as an institution. I respect the men on it. But I think that some of our courts, including this one, in recent years have gone too far in decisions that are weakening the peace forces as against the criminal forces, and I think we have to restore a proper balance.

Beyond that, we need better trained and better paid police. We need a reform of our prison system, and this must go very far. We need also to give our peace forces more adequate facilities—including wire-tapping authority, very carefully protected so it will not be abused—so that the peace forces will at least not be at a disadvantage against the criminal forces. Let's have a real war on crime in America so that the streets in our cities may be safe again. It can happen, and I pledge that we will have that kind of a war in this country.

Would you continue J. Edgar Hoover—Mr. FBI himself—in office, assuming that both you and he feel he will continue to be able to serve?

Some of the candidates on the campaign trail have said that Mr. Hoover has outlived his usefulness, and that they would replace him. I don't know what Mr. Hoover's plans are, what he wants to do about serving under the next President. But having known him for 21 years, I do know this: He has been a man who has kept the FBI, the most powerful police force in the world, out of politics. That is the *kind of man* we need as head of the FBI. That's the *kind of man* I will have as head of the FBI, if I have the opportunity to make that decision.

What are your views on the war in Vietnam? How do you propose to stop it? Should we pull out, or what?

I have expressed my views on Vietnam many times. At the present time, I am not able to express my views as completely as I otherwise would because of the negotiations right now going on in Paris.

We all want to bring this war to an honorable conclusion as quickly as possible. The only man at this time who has a chance to negotiate that kind of a settlement is President Johnson, with his advisers. Under those circumstances, I say that as long as there is a chance that he could be able to negotiate such a settlement—even though prospects at this moment do not seem too hopeful—let's not have any political figure in this country making statements that would lead the enemy to believe that he could get a different kind of a deal by waiting and not dealing with President Johnson. In other words, let's not destroy the chance for a peaceful settlement by a mouthful of words.

What would you do, as President, if North Vietnam walks out of the Paris talks?

I'm not trying to dodge that question, but if I were to say what I'd do, I would be giving away the game in advance. Any man who is running for President, and who says I would do this or that if North Vietnam does this or that, he is in effect sending a message to North Vietnam that might induce them to walk out.

What I'm trying to get across is this. I have sat in conferences where decisions were made that determined the difference between war and peace. And I have negotiated settlements—for example, the end of the steel strike in 1959. And I know it is tremendously important that whoever is doing the negotiating must not have the ground cut out from under him. We have a united front on negotiation in Paris now—I'm not going to open a second front politically, here in the United States of America, that would make the job more difficult. I say let's give President Johnson a reasonable time—I don't mean an indefinite time, but a reasonable time—to negotiate an honorable settlement. On that, he has the backing of the American people, who are united in their desire for peace, an honorable peace. But I don't mean to suggest by this that we're going to wait indefinitely.

I think also the American people believe we've gone the extra mile by stopping most of the bombing of North Vietnam in order to get the North Vietnamese to come to the conference table. They could make no greater miscalculation than to think that by increasing the temper of the war, by delaying, by belligerent talk, they're going to blackmail the United States and its President into accepting any settlement which is dishonorable. Let's make that very clear.

How do you feel about lowering the voting age to 18?

I'm for it—and not just because I carried Kentucky in 1960, which had the 18-year-old vote even then. I'm for it, however, for a different reason than the one given by some other candidates, who have said: if you're old enough to fight, then you're old enough to vote. That isn't a very good reason. The better reason is this: if you're smart enough, *then* you're old enough certainly to vote. And as I look at the 18-year-olds today, they *are* smarter, they are better qualified, they know more about politics in the world than did the 21-year-olds and 22-year-olds 30 years ago. For that reason, I say, let's let the 18-year-olds vote.

What do you think of the Poor People's March on Washington?

We should have nothing but sympathy for those in this nation who are poor, and those who participated in the march for that reason. However, those who say they are going to Washington for the purpose of getting more federal funds for welfare or the dole, I think they are missing the mark. What we need at the present time, as far as all Americans are concerned, are not more millions on welfare rolls but more millions on pay-rolls. I think we need that kind of policy in order to solve this problem and accomplish the real objective of the poor people, which is to stop being poor.

As for those who did march to Washington, they have been and should be listened to sympathetically. Certainly the Congress of the United States will pay attention to their petitions. But on the other hand, the Congress of the United States should not, and cannot, legislate behind a barricade. Let's make our decisions, but let's not make them on the basis of violence or threats. Let us make them on the basis of reason, and we'll have a better country for all Americans.

If you win the Republican nomination, will you debate with the Democratic nominee?

Well, I suppose many of my supporters—and obviously we do have some—will be thinking, "I hope he says no!"

I want to make one thing clear. I believe a man must be tested. That is why, when I decided to become a candidate for President, I decided first to go down that long, hard road of the primaries. That is why I'm here answering questions. As far as debates are concerned, I think the presidential candidates of the two major parties should debate—but only if legislation can be passed which will limit it to the two, and so avoid the "equal time" requirement that would otherwise oblige the television networks to open up their news coverage to endless hours of political debate by minor challengers. But if the two major candidates could meet each other in a proper format, and debate, I would certainly welcome the opportunity to do so. And, incidentally, I think I'll do a lot better than I did in those 1960 debates.

As President, would you continue or discontinue such Democratic programs as Headstart, Follow-Through, and the Job Corps?

First of all, Headstart was a Republican program, rather than a Democratic one. But that doesn't mean that partisanship should enter into any kind of a program that is worthwhile. I would continue Headstart. It takes the children at a time, in their formative years, when if they are lost they will be lost forever. Let's give the children a chance, which Headstart is giving them. That is one program that I believe deserves continuing and could even be increased.

As far as the Job Corps is concerned, I think that is one that has been a failure. Let me tell you why. It sounds good, but it costs $10,000 a year to train a man for a job that may not even exist. That's the government way of doing it. I say there is a better way. I say let's give a tax credit to private enterprise to train the unemployed for jobs that really exist. That's the way to get at the unemployment problem, not a federal Job Corps program, in my opinion.

How do you feel about compulsory military training—the draft?

I believe our present draft system is obsolete. And I believe that one of the dividends of peace after the war in Vietnam must be to abolish the draft and to substitute for it a volunteer armed forces system. I say that for several reasons. First, as far as any future wars of the United States are concerned—and I trust we can develop policies that will avoid any future war—it's either going to be world war, a nuclear war, in which you will not need mass armies. Or it will be a small war like we have in Vietnam, a guerrilla war, which requires a highly trained professional armed force and a highly trained professional civilian force. These are what the United States must prepare for. But the draft just isn't fitted for either kind of war.

So I say let's abolish the draft, let's not have that hanging over the lives of our young people. And then let's raise the pay of our armed forces so that we can have a highly trained, highly skilled professional force. That's what we ought to do.

What would a Nixon administration do about the Cuban situation—a communist base 90 miles from our shores?

The Cuban situation is at a point where, unfortunately, we cannot do now what we could have done earlier. Let me put it this way. As a result of our failure to move in at the time of the Bay of Pigs invasion in 1961, and as a result of our failure to use our power effectively during the Cuban missile confrontation in 1962, we're in a position now where to mount any kind of a military operation would be extremely difficult, and extremely hazardous, and might risk a confrontation with the Soviet Union.

On the other hand, there are some things we *can* do now. I think what we must do is to maintain and tighten the economic blockade on Castro's Cuba. In addition to that, I think we should encourage those individuals outside of Cuba who do not support that Cuban government—encourage them, that is, by being willing to discuss with them what could happen in the future, the possibilities of U.S. cooperation after the fact, in the event that the Castro regime were to come down. At this time, however, for anyone to say, "If I'm elected President I will move in on Cuba," would be unrealistic. Because of the mistakes of the past, it cannot be done. This doesn't mean that we are writing off the Cuban people. This doesn't mean that we are accepting Castro as being inevitably there. It does mean that we have to find other areas, economic and diplomatic, other than military, in order to effect a change in the Cuban regime.

What is your position on social security?

As a congressman, as a senator, as vice president of the United States, and as a candidate for President, I supported social security and the increases for social security. I supported the legislation in the Eisenhower Administration in which we expanded social security coverage to millions who hadn't had it previously. I supported it then—I support it now. Let me say that I not only favor it, I think in this rich country we can and should provide more effectively for our older people, also for those among us who are disabled and unable to earn a living.

But there's one thing we will do that this administration has not done. Because the people living on social security have a fixed income, they are the ones who have suffered the most in the rise in prices. They have seen their grocery bills go up, and their clothing bills go up, and their rent go up. And I say if I am elected President, not only will we keep social security, we will stop the rise in prices, which for many people is reducing their social security benefits through this hidden tax of cruel inflation.

Do you favor the proposal Governor Rockefeller has made for compulsory health insurance?

No, I do not favor compulsory health insurance for all Americans. All you have to do is look around the world, look where it has been tried. England, for example, has compulsory health insurance. What has it done? Well, it provides medical care for all Britishers, but it has reduced the standard of that care. As a result, many Britishers come to the United States in order to get what we have here: the *best* medical care in the world. Now, I do favor the kind of programs that provide medical care for the aged, for those in need, all that. But when it comes to compulsory health insurance, I think everyone should have the right to make his own decision, and have his own family doctor, and I therefore oppose compulsory health insurance for Americans who do not want it.

Why and how did you enter politics?

Well, that was many years ago. My story is a hard one to believe because the first public office I ever ran for was the Congress of the United States. I was only 32 years of age at the time, and I had just come out of the Navy. In the congressional district where I lived—it was the 12th Congressional District of California—we had a five-term Congressman, Jerry Voorhis, a very able man, a very well known man, a very liberal man, more liberal certainly than the district was at that time. The people of that district, many of the leaders, did a very unusual thing. They needed a candidate to run against Voorhis, and they had trouble getting one because nobody had been able to run close to him before. So they indicated in a press release that anybody who wanted to run for Congress could appear before a committee of 100 interested citizens and have an opportunity perhaps to get the committee's endorsement and run for Congress.

A hometown friend of mine, Herman Perry, a banker, he has since died, wired me at Middle River, Md., where I was a Lieutenant Commander of the Navy settling contracts. He wired me and said, would you like to come out and run for Congress? Well, I talked to Pat, my wife, about it, and she agreed that I should do it. I don't know if she has regrets now, but at least she agreed then. I flew out and appeared before the committee. I made a 12-minute speech, and as a result of that 12-minute speech I got the endorsement of the committee, I won the election for the Congress of the United States, and kept winning for a long time before I lost my first election in 1960.

Would you recommend any economic or military assistance to Israel? Would you continue economic assistance to Egypt?

This opens up a question which, next to Vietnam, is the most serious foreign policy question in the world today. For, if the war in Vietnam is brought to a conclusion, the place where war is most likely to break out again is in the Middle East. Now, as far as Israel is concerned, it is essential that she maintain the military strength which will discourage her neighbors from threatening or attacking her. Let's understand, once and for all: Israel is not trying to drive the other nations on her perimeter into the sea. It's those nations, Nasser and his colleagues, who are trying to drive Israel into the sea. Therefore, in order to avoid and to reduce the possibility of further war—a war of revenge launched by Nasser and the others —it is essential for Israel to maintain her military strength. And we should help the Israelis to maintain it, if that is necessary.

Further, I would simply say this. Looking at the

Mid-East, we need a whole new approach, a new general policy. We need to encourage and support what I would call the "moderate" Arab leaders—who may bring some influence to bear on Nasser. Nasser, of course, is the key to it, because he's the strongest leader. I don't believe that we should simply write him off. Unless we can communicate with Nasser, open a dialogue with him, the danger of his launching an attack on Israel sometime in the future still remains. But I think that we've made a mistake in not helping the other Arab states in the area, the moderate states, more than we have.

Would you cut federal spending? If so, where would you cut it?

Yes, I would cut federal spending. As to where precisely the budget should be cut, that is not the province of somebody who is outside the government, nor even the province of somebody who is in Congress. We can indicate *areas*. For example, we should not cut social security. We should not cut those who are receiving benefits because of need. On the other hand, we can defer some public works projects; we can defer some space programs; we can make cuts in the non-essential areas which can be postponed. Personnel could be cut in many areas. For example, we could cut 50 percent in most of our foreign personnel abroad, and still do a better job. I say that based on observations made during my travels to over 40 countries in the last four years.

But where precisely the cuts should be made in the current budget, only one man can tell us—that is President Johnson. He's the chief executive officer of this country, he has access to the Bureau of the Budget, he knows where the fat is. I say it's time again for him to step up and bite this bullet and tell us where to cut, and then Congress will follow. I will support what cuts he recommends.

Who would you like as a running mate?

You'd be surprised at how often I'm asked that question, as I go around the country, and I'm sure the other presidential candidates get it too. Let me answer it in this way. I will not make a decision on that question until we get to the convention and it becomes apparent that I may be the nominee. At that time, I will meet with our major party leaders from around the country and get their views on two issues: 1) which man, of all those available for the vice presidency, they think is best qualified, in case of need, to become President—that's the most important factor. And, 2) which man they think would be the best candidate in their state. Then, after I get the advice of all my friends and others, I will make the decision.

I want to say one final thing on this point. As a result of what President Eisenhower did in upgrading the vice presidency when I was vice president, and as a result of what President John F. Kennedy did along the same lines later, the vice presidency today is so important that it can no longer be used simply to balance a ticket geographically or ideologically. I want the man for vice president who, if something would happen to me, would make the best President of the United States.

Do you agree with Mayor Richard Daley of Chicago, who said that to stop riots in city streets the police should shoot to kill?
If not, how are we going to stop such riots?

I think there has been too much oversimplified talk on how you stop riots. What Mayor Daley said was that the police should shoot arsonists and looters, and a lot of people applauded this statement. Why not? Arsonists are committing crimes, and so are looters.

Now here is my answer. I believe that when you see a riot coming up, what you need first of all is to have an adequate amount of force in the area—I mean by that security forces, armed forces if necessary—to discourage any who might engage in illegal action. Then, if they do engage in illegal action, you have to be quite precise in your use of that force. Now in the case of arson, you are dealing with possible murder. Anybody that goes out, starts a fire to burn down a house or a shop, he might kill somebody, and that is why where an arsonist is concerned I would give police forces the right, the responsibility, to use whatever force is necessary, including firearms, to stop that potential murderer.

But now let us look at a looter---say these 13, 14 or 15-year-old children who dashed into the streets and picked up a loaf of bread, or carried a pair of shoes

out of the store. This is unarmed robbery, and we don't use firearms for an unarmed robbery. They should be arrested, of course. You should try to stop it in that way. If you were to use firearms on looters, what it might do is explode a small riot into a much bigger one, or into a real racial holocaust.

Now, how do we stop riots over the long haul? What we have to do is, first, to see that the law is enforced strictly whenever any violation occurs, and also to see that adequate force is available when we have any incipient riots and violence. Second, we have got to have an early warning system. Many of those who live in these communities are developing that kind of system, so that we can knock down the inflammatory rumors in advance before they blow up into big trouble. Third, what we have to do of course is to get at some of the causes. That is a longer range problem. I have made several speeches recently on the subject, "Bridges to Human Dignity," in which the real causes of the riots are examined and the cures. And one of those cures is to get, within the ghettos, more people who have an *interest* in the system—people for example who own their homes, people who operate their own shops. Once a person has an interest in the American system, then he is going to be the one that is going to take steps to stop the riots. So that's the long range answer to stop the riots.

Can you win in November regardless of who is the Democratic nominee?

When Democratic candidates tell you that they can bring new leadership to America they do not tell you that each one of them is tied to the policies of the past. They helped to make the policies.

Now as I travel across the United States there is one thing that comes through loud and clear. The American people believe we're in deep trouble at home and abroad. They think we need a change. They think it should be a real change; not just a change of face.

The American people believe we need a change of policy, and I say that when the American people go to the polls to vote they're not going to vote for somebody who supported the policies that got us into trouble. They're going to vote for a new man who can give us a new policy—and that's what I pledge to give to the American people.

How do you stand on Communist China and the United Nations? Should we try to bring them into the UN?

In Communist China today we have 700,000,000 people, and by the end of this century there will be a billion and a half people living there, with an immense nuclear capability. To suggest that the United States follow a policy of choosing to have no dialogue and no communication with Communist China would be, of course, a very irresponsible thing. As for the next President, one of his major tasks in his first term—and certainly in his second term if not in his first—would be to create the conditions whereby we can open communication with Communist China, and try to bring them around at least to the point of view of the Soviet Union—which, while still causing us plenty of trouble in the Middle East and other places, has at least given up the idea of a nuclear confrontation. In other words, what we need to do is create an area of strength around China, from Japan clear around to India, which will contain its expansion so that Communist China will turn inward rather than outward. That is the long-range goal.

As for the short-range goal—we should not now under any circumstances, recognize Communist China, admit it to the U.N. or trade with it, because that nation at the present time is an outlaw nation. And if at a time when Communist China is causing trouble in India, and when it is threatening a number of nations around its perimeter, when it is violating all of the precepts of the United Nations—if at such a time we admitted it to the United Nations, it would destroy the United Nations. Therefore, I would oppose it at this time.

What are the points of difference between you and Rockefeller, and between you and Reagan?

I noted, at one point last May, Governor Nelson A. Rockefeller made a statement to the effect that he didn't have any substantial philosophical differences with Governor Ronald Reagan. Later, however, he modified that statement.

I suppose that, in answering this question, I'm expected to say, well, I don't have any differences with either of these men. But that isn't true. I have several differences with Governor Rockefeller, and several with Governor Reagan, as they have with me.

And that's what our two-party system is about. In a country which has just two major parties, there's got to be room inside each of them for people who have differences. Otherwise, you have the kind of fragmentized, many-party system that led to the French problem, where to keep things going DeGaulle finally had to step in and take over with virtually one-party rule. I want to make one thing clear. The differences I have with Governor Reagan and with Governor Rockefeller, or with any of my Republican friends, are infinitesimal compared to the differences I have with Eugene McCarthy or Hubert Humphrey, and that's why I say let's get together.

I'd go a step further, when you say why don't you tell us what the differences are. I think the debate this year should take place not between Republicans, but with our Democratic opponents. Let's make it clear that together, as Republicans, we can present at Miami a platform that will provide plenty of room for everybody to get on it, and at the same time plenty of room for Democrats—millions of them—to get on it too because they will realize that we offer the best hope for new leadership. That's what we want to do.

What do you think of Vice President Hubert Humphrey as a possible Presidential candidate and opponent?

I've known Hubert Humphrey for a number of years, almost 20 years. I respect him as a hard-working public servant. I completely disagree with his political philosophy in many respects. We've had some vigorous debates from time to time, both in the Senate and in the country. As to whether or not I think that he would be the Democrats' best candidate, I have some ideas on that, but I'm not going to tell them.

Are you in favor of repealing 14-B, the part of the Taft-Hartley law which lets each state decide for itself whether to allow the "union shop" or "closed shop"?

Twenty years ago, when I was on the labor committee of the House of Representatives, I helped to write the Taft-Hartley Act. I particularly helped to write—along with Congressman McKinnen of Minnesota—Section 14-B. This is the section which leaves to the state the right to determine what the rules

NIXON ON THE NEED FOR ORDER

Richard Nixon has spoken out on the need for order in our society—the number one domestic issue of our time.

Crime has become a first priority domestic crisis, a distinct threat to the social order, and it should be a matter of the highest Federal urgency.

"

In a free and open society where there are legal and peaceful means for change and progress, there is no cause that justifies going outside the law and no cause that justifies resort to violence.

"

Organized crime is the tapeworm of the American society. In recent years it has prospered as never before and broadened its influence in government and legitimate business and unions.

"

We cannot explain away crime in this country by charging it off to poverty. The role of poverty as a cause of the crime upsurge has been grossly exaggerated.

"

One of the operative principles of a free society is that men are accountable for what they do. No criminal can justify his crimes on the basis of some real or imagined grievance against society.

"

If the American people are willing to commit themselves to the proposition that any man who disobeys the law pays the penalty the law exacts, then we can reduce crime by making it a more hazardous and less rewarding occupation.

"

Under the Constitution of the United States we are guaranteed the right to disagree, not the right to disobey the laws of our land.

"

Academic freedom is not academic anarchy. The student who deliberately stops the process of education to make his point of protest is denying academic freedom to his fellow students.

"

should be with regard to "union security." And which provides that each state shall have the right to declare whether, within that state, a man has to join a union in order to have a job. Those who advocate repealing 14-B would in effect prefer the federal government to have that power, and would deny to the states the right to have their own rules.

I believe that 14-B should not be repealed. I believed it was a good provision 20 years ago, I think it's a good provision today. We've had too much of a tendency to get the federal government to take over. Today, rather than have the states give up any more power to the federal government, we should have Washington giving more power to the states. That's what I believe.

I heard the evangelist Billy Graham say the other night that he was a friend of yours. I would like to know, what kind of an individual is he?

You know, here's an interesting thing. I've been noticing what we call crowdsmanship in the political campaigns, with each candidate claiming he is getting bigger crowds than any of the others. You know we all play that game. But one thing we've got to admit: the champion at drawing crowds is Billy Graham. Here in Oregon while I've been campaigning in the primary, Billy Graham has been holding a series of his religious meetings in Portland, and I noticed he was getting 20,000 to 25,000 people for each meeting. That means something—and I'll tell you what I think it means. I think there is a deep longing among the American people today for a return to spiritual and moral values. Now many of them may not support Billy Graham's approach, but they do support what he's trying to do. He is stirring the American people. He is reaching their hearts and their souls and their minds with his great appeal.

Now, what kind of man is he? I know him quite well. I've known him, going back almost 20 years. I played golf with him, and when you play golf with a man you get to know very well what kind of a fellow he is. Incidentally, he's a much better golfer than I am. Billy Graham is a sincere man. In personal conversation he is very exciting, and not just a one-track man with a one-track mind. He can talk about politics, about sports, about physical fitness—his interests are very broad. He has traveled the world. He has a deep understanding of people, and that is the reason, I think, why he has a great appeal in his ministry. Beyond that, I want to say that in these days when we hear that everything's phony, that some people even think an evangelist must be a phony, making money on the side and all the rest, I can say for Billy Graham—speaking as just one man who knows him—he's a very sincere, deeply dedicated, Christian man, and he's a great credit to America here and in the world.

When the garbage workers struck in New York City a few months ago, Mayor John Lindsay wasn't about to concede on points of principle. But Governor Rockefeller thought the most important thing was to get garbage collection started again, even if the price was a stiff one. Where did you stand on this issue?

It was a difficult matter for the Mayor and for the Governor, and I know that both men were very sincere in their attempt to find an answer. But I think that Mayor Lindsay was right and the Governor was wrong. Now the reason for that is, where you have a strike by public employes, I just don't believe you can justify it. I believe that those who work for government should have procedures to allow them to negotiate so they can keep up—so that, in compensation, they don't fall behind organized labor working for private industry. But I don't believe that when you talk about teachers striking, for example, or our sanitation workers striking, or policemen striking, or firemen striking—I don't believe that the education of our children, or the health of our people, or the safety of our streets can be put on the collective-bargaining table as hostages. I am against that kind of a strike. And for that reason I think the mayor was right in his approach as compared with the governor in this instance.

Is it true that you live in the same New York apartment house where Governor Rockefeller lives?

Yes I do, as a matter of fact. Where there is a difference is, his apartment is considerably bigger than mine. Some people, I suppose, would think I should feel a little, you know, envious about it, but I don't. As a matter of fact I talked it over with Pat, my wife, and my two daughters here, and we decided we don't like an apartment too well, so we think maybe next year we'd like to move into a house—if you'll help us.

Some of the packages I've sent and received through the mail recently have been disgracefully handled. Do you think anything can be done to improve the postal service?

Well, I know one thing you can do. There are several months left till election. You work as hard as you can for the election of a new Republican President, and we'll improve that postal service! We'll see that your packages are well taken care of.

No, seriously, the postal service *has* deteriorated terribly. Part of it is the great increase in traffic, but part of it is pure politics. The Post Office department, very frankly, has been used too much as a political football, as a place to reward faithful political people. The Post Office needs to be run like a first-class business, and I can assure you that one of the top priorities I have on my agenda if I have the opportunity to serve is to get a Postmaster General who will not be just a political man, but who will be able to institute the reforms that will give the American people the kind of postal service they're paying for. Because they are paying enough. We're just not providing the service that we should.

Is it possible to reduce foreign aid and still maintain our influence in the world?

Not only is it possible, it is necessary. Let's look at American foreign aid. I supported it when I was a congressman 21 years ago, immediately after World War II. I thought it was necessary and important then. But since that time we have spent over 150 billion dollars helping the countries of Europe and others around the world through foreign aid. Now many of the countries we have helped are rich and strong and able to help themselves, and I say that it's time we had a new foreign policy, in which other nations share more heavily than they do in foreign aid, so that the United States doesn't have to carry the major burden that it's been carrying for much too long. I pledge that kind of policy as President.

Stellar Campaign Team—*Dick, Julie, Tricia and Pat*

This is a personal question.
How do you keep your weight down?

Well, it isn't easy. But I have very strong arms, you know—I just push the food back. I wish there were another way. Exercise? Yes, for physical fitness, but let me tell you what it does to me: the more I exercise the more I eat, and then I gain more, so as far as keeping weight down is concerned, exercise doesn't help me. As for foods, I do without the usual things; starches, for example. I don't eat any desserts, and I love desserts. And I see my wife Pat—you know she loves those potatoes and she eats them down and doesn't gain a pound, and I can't even touch them.

What do I eat, then? Well, proteins. And cottage cheese—I eat cottage cheese till it runs out of my ears. But I've learned a way to eat it that makes it not too bad. I put ketchup on it. At least that way it doesn't taste like cottage cheese. I'll tell you where I learned that—from my grandmother. My grandmother lived to be 91 years of age, and she always mixed ketchup with her cottage cheese.

And I might add one thing. Running for the Presidency helps keep your weight down, too.

In view of the current tax increase, budget deficits, and inflation, what is your opinion on continuing the race to the moon?

I believe that the race to the moon must take a lower priority, at this time, than saving the American dollar and—putting it quite bluntly—rescuing the budget of millions of Americans throughout this country. Now, I do favor the exploration of space. As many of you will remember, in the Eisenhower administration I was somewhat in a minority, as one of those who was advocating the space program. I still believe in it. As President of the United States I would certainly go forward with the space program, from the funds available. And I believe we will be second to none.

What would you do about the Pueblo and its crew, the U.S. Navy ship seized and now being held by the communist North Koreans?

When you ask about the *Pueblo,* you're asking me, in effect, how do you lock the barn door after the horse is stolen? What happened was that the *Pueblo,* this American naval vessel, was in international waters off Korea for weeks before it was seized. During that time the North Koreans harassed it, they threatened it, and our government, for reasons I will never understand, failed to send a destroyer in, failed to provide cover in any way to protect it. And so as a result the North Koreans—an outlaw government—seized the *Pueblo.* And now they have the *Pueblo,* and not just the ship: they have 83 Americans. They are hostages.

Now I could say to you, what you do to get the *Pueblo* back is to move right in. But the moment we moved right in, 83 Americans would be dead. And just getting back that ship or killing some North Koreans, it seems to me, would serve no purpose at all at this point. What we have to do now, what we are reduced to, is to use whatever diplomatic means we can, through the Soviet Union and otherwise, that might have some leverage in North Korea. But I do say this: It should never have happened in the first place, and I can assure you that as President I will see to it that it will never happen again.

Now I want to tell you why it happened in the first place: Because we didn't listen to the warnings. This is not an incident that just occurred, just like that. Look what has happened to respect for the United States all over the world. You have to realize that for the past five years we have seen more incidents of our embassies being stoned, and our libraries being burned, and our ambassadors being insulted, and one consul general being made to eat the flag in one case—and the flag has been spit upon and torn in other places. Around the world again and again and again we have seen that sort of thing, and the government does nothing to deal with it. This means that small nations and big ones as well get more and more . . . courageous, shall we say, and finally an incident like the seizure of the *Pueblo* occurs.

I simply want to state, as I have stated to audiences all over this nation: I believe that when respect for this country, the biggest nation of the world—I should say the strongest—and the richest nation—when respect for the United States has been allowed to fall so low that a little power like North Korea will seize an American naval vessel on the high seas, then it's time for new leadership in the White House, to restore respect for the United States.   END

Proud Dad, Glad Grad and Pat Nixon, LL.D.—*Two days before Father's Day, June 14th, 1968, Tricia Nixon received her B.A. degree from Finch College in New York and Pat was awarded an honorary Doctorate in law. The former Vice President delivered the commencement address*

Telethonic Talent in Oregon— *Tricia and Julie Nixon answe*
phones during Dad's telethon, relaying questions to program moderator Bu
Wilkinson (former college football coach and longtime Nixon friend

NIXON NOTES

I believe in the American dream because I have seen it come true in my own life.

Politics as usual is not enough for America today. Diplomacy as usual is not enough for the world today. We need new leadership. We need new ideas.

The present administration's approach is to begin with the government. Ours is to begin with people.

Whenever I can get private enterprise in on the job, I know that it will do it more efficiently and faster.

We need the same energy in positive causes that negative causes enlist. We need helping hands, not marching feet.

Our opinion makers have gone too far in promoting the doctrine that when a law is broken, society, not the criminal, is to blame.

Worse than not keeping a promise is making a promise that cannot be kept. Much of the bitterness of the Negro slum dweller is the result of these false promises.

The problems of the cities should not blind us to the problems of rural America, with its fifty million people.

We must make welfare payments a temporary expedient, not a permanent way of life; something to be escaped from, not to.

This generation is neither 'lost' nor 'beat'; it is lonely, partly due to the natural rebelliousness of youth, but due largely to an outdated paternalism on the part of our national leaders.

Richard M. Nixon

THE ROAD AHEAD

Toward An
Expanding Democracy

"If there is one thing common to all groups, all races, all ages in America today, it is this: a deep feeling that they want to be a part of things, to have a say in things, to have a voice and to have that voice heard."

TOWARD AN EXPANDING DEMOCRACY

During the past five months I've campaigned in twenty-two states, and talked with thousands of people from every walk of life. I've had a chance to sense the mood of America, in the way that only a candidate who goes to the people senses it.

And I've found something.

I've found an anxiety about the future, and about the place of the individual—who more and more seems alone and powerless.

Through this anxiety, there runs a common thread: that society in the mass is losing touch with the individual in the flesh; that the sense of community—of a place of belonging where leaders listen and respond—has crumbled; that the power to control decisions immediately affecting one's life is vanishing; that that unique, precious, indescribable thing—the individual human mind, heart and spirit—is being injured, or neglected, or slighted.

If we listen, we'll discover that the white man in the Boston suburbs shares many of the same frustrations as the black man in the Chicago Ghetto. Not all, of course. But he, too, wants to be heard. He too, wants a voice in the decisions that shape his life.

Those protesting college students who carry signs reading: "Do not fold, bend, staple or mutilate. This is a human being," speak not only for the student revolt, but for the frustrations of Americans everywhere.

Beyond the disorders, there's another rebellion going on today. This other is a quiet revolution. In part, it is a protest against the violence and the excesses that have marked a time of tumultuous change. It is a protest against the heavier-and-heavier demands of an age of impatience.

It's a rebellion against taxes, against the ever-higher piling of Federal tax on state tax on local tax.

It's a demand for moderation—moderation in the tone of public discourse, in the style of public protest, in the posturing and promises of public officials.

It's also something more.

The people who make up this great quiet majority want a voice in the shaping of their own future. They're not against change; what they want is to participate in the process of change, to help mold the future to their own designs rather than be swept along by impersonal forces.

In fact, if there is one thing common to all groups, all races, all ages, in America today, it is this: a deep, gut feeling that they want to be a part of things, to have a say in things, to have a voice—and to have that voice heard.

When we look closely, we see that much of what is lacking in our society today is precisely what America was established to provide.

Ours was conceived, in the eloquent simplicity of Lincoln's words, as a "government of the people, by the people and for the people."

As we look back over this middle third of the century, we find that we have been getting more and more government for the people, but less and less government of the people and by the people.

In this lies the root of much of today's frustration.

Roots of Disorder

As everything around him has gotten bigger, the individual has gotten smaller by comparison. He's been lost in the mass of things, his voice drowned out in the chorus.

The machinery of government seems increasingly remote, increasingly incapable of meeting his needs when action is needed. The community itself begins to appear less relevant, and its standards and restraints become less effective.

One reason people are shouting so loudly today is that it's so far from where they are to where the power is. If we fail to bring power closer—if we persist in treating complex local needs from remote centers—we'll be repeating tomorrow mistakes that already have added dangerously to the frictions of today.

Revolution of Ideas

Can we do anything about the frustrations that the alienated and the rest of us share? There's no doubt in my mind that we can.

Among many of our leading thinkers, there's been another quiet revolution going on—a revolution of ideas about the way the nation should be organized to deal with its problems.

After a third of a century of concentrating power, an old idea is winning a new acceptance: the idea that what we need is a dispersal of power. What we need is not one leader, but many leaders; not one center of power, but many centers of power.

Richard Goodwin stated this proposition cogently: "Whatever our particular position, the one overriding goal of political life must be to help restore and strengthen that faith of the individual in himself which is the source of national direction and generosity of deed."

This is a concept in which I deeply believe.

It also is the clearest-cut issue of this year's Presidential campaign.

The man who is most likely to be nominated by the Democratic party—Vice President Humphrey—is a man I respect. He is a man of honor and a man of his convictions. And he honestly believes in the old ways. I believe in a new way.

Power has been flowing to Washington for a third of a century, and now it's time to start it flowing back —to the states, to the communities, and most important, to the people.

Every program I offer in this campaign will be tested against this standard: Does it increase the power of the people, or diminish it? Does it enhance the self-respect, the pride, of the individual human being, or reduce it?

Time to Modernize

We now are at a great turning point. We have to decide which way to go: whether to take the old road that leads to a government getting bigger, and bigger, and more and more impersonal—the road that leads to more rebellions, more frustrations—or whether we take a new road.

Every idea has its time. And the time is now for the idea of an expanded democracy, of moving government closer to the people, of breaking massive problems into manageable pieces. This way the people can participate, they can be involved, their voices can be heard and heeded.

It's time to think anew and act anew.

One of the first tasks of the next President should be to set in motion a searching, fundamental reappraisal of our whole structure of government—not only of the Federal departments and agencies, but also of state and local government, and its relation to the Federal structure.

Broad Mandate

I propose that we should establish a Commission on Government Re-Organization. This would be a commission with a difference. It would have a far broader mandate than those given the earlier Hoover Commissions.

It would thoroughly study ways of increasing the efficiency of government organization. But its focus would be equally on the responsiveness of government.

Toward this end, it would be charged with searching out every feasible means of decentralizing government, of getting it closer to the people, of transferring functions to state and local governments, of creating new instrumentalities where appropriate to involve the people at the community level directly in the decisions that affect their own lives.

It would seek new ways to transfer functions from government to private enterprise, and also to the great, vital voluntary sector—to enlist the energies of those millions of Americans who stand ready to serve and to help, in the best American tradition.

I have said that if I were President, I would give the Vice President major additional duties in helping administer the domestic functions of government. One of the first of these duties would be to involve himself directly in this entire effort to move government to the people, and make it more responsive.

Enlisting Energies

In turning away from ever bigger government we are not turning our backs on ever bigger problems. Our aim is not to ignore the problems, but to solve them. It's not to neglect the poor, but to serve their needs. It's not to sit idly by while our air and water are polluted, but to establish the most direct and effective means of control. It's not to give up in despair at snarled transportation, but to straighten out the snarl.

As we turn away from the old paternalism of the 40's and toward the expanded democracy of the 70's, we'll discover a new dignity, a new unity, a new stability in America. We'll discover anew that this land is our land, all of us together, that its destiny is our destiny. We are one nation, together and inseparable, and if that proposition has been tested in these past years, tested in the fires of our cities, tested in war and in the bitter debates the war engendered, tested in demonstrations and civil disobedience and in the wondering conflict of the generations, the nation has shown that it can pass that test. Despite our troubles, there's a gathering today of the forces that are going to cement our society back together again—determined that decency and justice will prevail, and determined that reason shall rule.

Emerson wrote that "governments have their origin in the moral identity of men." Woodrow Wilson

told us: "I believe in democracy because it releases the energy of every human being."

To make its expanded democracy work, America will need the willing hands of millions of individual people—proclaiming by their deeds that moral identity which is the rock our freedom rests on. America will need their involvement. It will need their ideas and their energies.

That is why, in this campaign, in this watershed year, I am asking not just for your votes in 1968, but for your continued help in the next Administration. That is why I ask not just your support, but also your enlistment in the great adventure on the road ahead.